For Greg

JESUS

AUTHORS TAKE SIDES

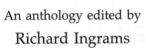

An anthology edited by
Richard Ingrams

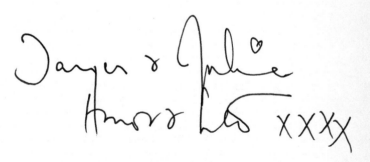

Happy Christmas 2012

all our love

Jasper & Juliet
Annorg Kato xxxx

HarperCollins*Publishers*

HarperCollins*Publishers*
77–85 Fulham Palace Road,
Hammersmith, London w6 8jb

Published by HarperCollins*Publishers* 1999
1 3 5 7 9 8 6 4 2

A catalogue record for this book is
available from the British Library

ISBN 0 00 255842 4

Set in PostScript Linotype Palatino by
Rowland Phototypesetting Ltd, Bury St Edmunds

Printed and bound in Great Britain by
Caledonian International Book Manufacturing Ltd, Glasgow

In memory of Andrew Osmond

Jesus of Nazareth sits in a chamber of every man's brain, immovable, immutable, however credited or discredited. The idea of Christ is the only inheritance that the rich have not stolen from the poor.

REBECCA WEST

The Young Rebecca

CONTENTS

INTRODUCTION

I have a vivid memory of sitting at the organ in church one Easter Sunday about twenty years ago and being struck by a phrase in the Gospel for the day (John, Chapter 20) – 'She supposing him to be the gardener . . .' The thought that occurred to me was that if, as some people claimed, the story of Jesus's resurrection was invented by the early church, it was a strange thing to suggest that when the risen Jesus first presented himself to Mary she mistook him for a gardener.

Was that the kind of thought that was likely to occur to me, a journalist, rather than a priest or theologian? Would a vicar be likely to preach a sermon on the text 'She supposing him to be the gardener?' I don't know. But that little revelation put into my head the idea that writers (and journalists, perhaps especially) look at the Bible in a different way from other people. That conviction was fortified when I read an interview which Graham Greene, a novelist but also, throughout his life, a journalist, gave to John Mortimer in which he too referred to the twentieth chapter of St John's Gospel. Greene based his conviction that it was an eye-witness account of what happened on the little details – the two disciples running to the tomb, John overtaking Peter and then being afraid to go into the tomb. 'It's like reportage,' he told his friend

Fr. Leopoldo Duran in a letter quoted in this book (p. 122).

As a magazine editor myself, I have spent many years looking at all kinds of writing submitted to me, having to decide whether it's any good or, as is often the case, whether it's factually true. As a book reviewer and biographer I have also had experience of assessing the value and importance of books, letters, diaries with a critical eye. Is it true? Do I believe it? Often one has nothing to go on apart from one's instinct.

In the case of the Gospels the same sort of situation applies. Despite the efforts of theologians and historians and other investigators to 'check out' the story by referring to the 'historical' evidence, there is no such evidence – no records, no inscriptions, no contemporaneous accounts with which to compare the stories of the four evangelists. Their narrative is all that we have to go on. Countless theologians have pored over those texts, detailing the discrepancies, comparing the different versions of different episodes with a scholarly precision. But might not the non-professional – the poet, novelist, critic, the journalist (even if he is not an orthodox believer) – have a more profound and thought-provoking insight into the story? It is on this basis that I have compiled this collection.

In *The Everlasting Man*, G.K. Chesterton (another journalist) asks us to imagine that we are reading the Gospels as newspaper stories. We would find them puzzling and terrifying, he says, just as the Christ of the Gospels 'might seem actually more strange and terrible than the Christ of the Church'. And it is easy to see why this should be so. The Church, in order to survive, laid stress only on what the Book of Common Prayer calls the 'comfortable words' of Jesus. It had to censor the story for the benefit of the faithful, many of whom could be easily alienated by what Stevie Smith calls the 'harsh ambiguous words', all the cruel elements in the story. This censorship applies not just to the more difficult parables – the story of the barren fig tree, the threats of hell and damnation – but to all those elements likely to offend important members of the congregation, such as the elevation of poverty and pacifism, or the apparent dismissal of the family as a valuable institution.

Yet it is precisely these 'difficult' elements in the story that writers are drawn to, some of them Doubting Thomases like Stevie Smith who find them an obstacle to belief, but others who, being no strangers to poverty and living rough, find Jesus appealing for the very reason that he seems to sanction their lifestyle. Of all the texts referred to here, the most popular is Matthew, Chapter 6: 'Consider the lilies of the field, how they grow; they toil not, neither do they spin ... Take therefore no thought for the morrow'.

In seeking an alternative emphasis such writers are following in a long political tradition which condemned the church for betraying Christ's teaching and aligning itself to the Establishment. These people had perverted the Gospel in order, as Carlyle put it, 'to keep silly men's souls in meshes of slavery and darkness'. Bishops were bracketed with kings and generals as the forces of reaction. Yet there was more to it than politics. The writer, as individualist, loner or even anarchist, found it hard to line up with an organization like the Church, while at the same time finding the story of its founder (another outsider) intensely moving and sympathetic.

We find this view still being articulated in our own time by, for example, the bohemian Paul Potts who says, 'I prefer the man I meet in the Gospels, to the God described in the work of theologians.' It is in the same spirit that the greatest of all novelists, Tolstoy (himself ex-communicated by the Russian Orthodox Church) did his best to define his own version of Christianity based on those teachings of Jesus which the Church had rejected or re-interpreted to appease the authorities. Others like Shelley or Shaw, who were not believers, painted a picture of Jesus as a reformer or, in some cases, a revolutionary. It is perhaps easy to sneer at this revisionism but others may find, as I do, the sincerely held opinions of non-believers more appealing than the hypocritical piety of the orthodox. In the same way William Blake, a believer, sided with the atheist Tom Paine (see p. 123) when he was attacked by the Church of England bishops for what was considered blasphemy. Thomas Hardy would seem to be the only great writer who questioned the authenticity of the Gospels (p. 98) though even he, apparently, liked to have the story of the Nativity read to him at Christmas time. Another poet, Robert Graves, is likewise alone in dismissing the New Testament as a poor piece of writing which has been dressed up in 'the glamour of early Jacobean prose'. Others, even the non-believers, are charmed by the narrative. 'Exceedingly affecting' is Dr Johnson's description of the forgiveness of Mary Magdalen; George Eliot finds the Road to Emmaus story 'most beautiful'; Oscar Wilde calls the Gospels 'four prose poems' and praises their 'freshness', 'naïvete' and 'simple romantic charm'. More recently, the critic Cyril Connolly, a man of no religious belief, is bowled over on reading St John's Gospel.

Then there is the huge scope for speculation which appeals to writers, many of whom have written novels and plays to fill in the gaps in the Gospel narrative – the most obvious being the lack of information about the first thirty years of Jesus's life. Even in the account of his final years the amount of information is tantalisingly little. So it is possible for William Blake to maintain that Jesus and his disciples were illiterate whilst his fellow poet, Robert Graves, insists that he was 'a man of unusual learning'. Opinions differ widely on the merits of the four evangelists. George Moore dismisses St Luke's account as 'a polished lifeless narrative'. John Cowper Powys calls it a drama equal to the Greek plays.

The evangelists also say nothing about Jesus's physical appearance – something that a professional writer finds frustrating. Many of them do their best to provide a picture. Carlyle rages at the painter Holman Hunt for showing Christ in his famous *Light of the World* as a dignified bearded man in a long white robe holding a lantern, the sort of figure who might appeal to Anglican churchmen but who bore no relation to the Christ Carlyle imagined: 'tired, hungry often and footsore, drinking at the spring, eating by the way, his rough and patched clothes bedraggled and covered with dust'. Norman Mailer, like Heine, reminds us that Christ was a Jew (another obvious fact that the Church was not keen to stress). On a more mundane level, Philip Toynbee, who spent many hours trying to imagine what Jesus was like, makes the obvious but curious point that he must have said a great many more things than those recorded in the Bible, such as 'I wonder what there'll be for supper' or 'I'm feeling a bit tired this morning.'

Not surprisingly there is a great deal of speculation about the miracle stories. The secularist non-believers like Shelley and Paine argue that these are invention and that the events described could not possibly have happened. William Cobbett, a great journalist and exposer of humbug, insists that the story is all of a piece and that you cannot separate scripture into 'false' and 'true'. Cobbett was by no means an orthodox believer, any more than Bernard Shaw who, following the lead of Rousseau, reminds us that Jesus had no wish to be recognised on account of his miracles and frequently told his disciples to keep quiet about them. Shaw himself, though not believing in the divinity of Christ, has no difficulty in believing in his miracles (any more than his fellow Irishman Oscar Wilde). 'There is as much evidence that the miracles occurred,' Shaw writes, 'as that the battle of Waterloo occurred.' While to Wilde the miracles seem 'as exquisite as the coming of spring and quite as natural'.

Shaw's opinion will surprise readers who think of him as the archetypal sceptic who would be inclined to agree with Tom Paine that 'the supernatural part [of the story] has every mark of fraud and imposition stamped upon the face of it.' Yet one of the points in a collection of this kind is to find unlikely people agreeing and disagreeing with one another. Thus Beverley Nichols, a writer despised and mocked by Graham Greene in his lifetime, makes an almost identical defence of the resurrection story to that of Greene already quoted. Shaw finds the idea of a married Jesus 'undignified'; D.H. Lawrence regards it as a weakness on his part that he was unable to come home, put his slippers on and 'sit under the spell of his wife'.

If there is any unanimity to be found in such a diverse collection it concerns the impact of Jesus's personality. Even those who reject his divinity (perhaps the majority of those quoted) find him an awe-inspiring figure. As Gerard Manley Hopkins says in his sermon (p. 136), 'Those even that do not follow, yet they look wistfully after him, own him a hero . . .' His fellow poet Keats, who like many of the Romantics rejected what he called 'the pious frauds of religion', sums up in a wonderful sentence, 'Yet through all this I see his splendour.' In so doing he and others seem to be echoing unconsciously the view of Jesus's contemporaries. John Stewart Collis fastens on the sentence, 'And Jesus went before them: and they were amazed.' John Updike, likewise, in a long review of St Matthew, comments 'Amazement prevails.'

In the same spirit, others prefer the emphasis of G.K. Chesterton whose overall impression of the Gospel is that it is 'in some ways a very strange story', like Jesus himself 'strange and terrible'. Stevie Smith refers to the 'strange parables', John Cowper Powys calls Jesus's wanderings a 'strange itinerary' when he tries to imagine the thoughts of someone coming to St Luke's Gospel without any preconceptions. Alice Thomas

Ellis considers 'the pagan gods pitifully dull and predictable in comparison with His strangeness'.

It is this emphasis on 'strangeness' that will itself seem strange to anyone for whom the figure of Jesus is, if anything, too familiar, even cosy – the smiling bearded Jesus described by Gerard Manley Hopkins, the Jesus of the Sunday-school picture and the stained glass window. Yet, by and large, the writers quoted here are not concerned, like some modern theologians, with trying to substitute a human figure for a divine or mythical one – in cutting Jesus down to size, in other words. Bernard Shaw's view of miracles is considerably more orthodox than that of many of today's bishops; while it would not be immediately obvious from reading Tolstoy's interpretation of the New Testament that he regarded it as blasphemous to believe that Christ was God. It was the same Tolstoy who dismissed as childish and contemptible Renan's *Life of Jesus*, the first of many attempts to discover a historical Jesus beneath the supposed myths and fables of the evangelists. George Eliot, who translated the massive *Life of Jesus* by the German theologian D.F. Strauss, was similarly scornful and found the whole business arduous and depressing, though again she herself was no longer a practising Christian.

There is no clear dividing line between believers and non-believers in this collection. The divinity of Jesus is either accepted or denied, but seldom discussed. Shaw speaks for many when he says that if Jesus was a supernatural figure he would lose all interest in him and is answered by Paul Verlaine insisting that he has no time for a merely human Jesus. More often than not it is difficult to tell from what they write precisely where particular writers stood on the question. It is as if, as far as many of them are concerned, they consider it a subject for theologians to argue about. (It is also true that the obsessions of the professional atheist – the mistakes and inconsistencies of the narratives, the apparent similarities between the story of Jesus and assorted pagan myths – are not shared by the majority of our writers.)

If all good writing – whether poetry, fiction, history or journalism – is in some way a search for truth, it should follow that when writers approach the New Testament they give us a more truthful insight than those who are in the business of religion – the priests and theologians who are obliged in their public utterances not to disturb the faithful. Not all the extracts quoted here will measure up to that high standard and many of them are more interesting for the light they throw on the author than on the character of Jesus. All the same, I believe that a collection like this can provide more nourishing food for thought than most books bearing the official *imprimatur* on the same subject, if only because it reflects the doubts and misgivings, as well as the sense of strangeness, that most of us feel when confronted by the stories.

It is a cliché that Christianity is dead, just as it is a cliché that England is no longer a Christian country. As we approach the two-thousandth anniversary of Jesus's birth there is a consensus that he no longer has much relevance – to use a keyword in modern jargon – to the generation of today. In a 'multi-faith society' it is claimed, all religions must be equally respected and Christianity given no special status. That may be a view that can be held by politicians and headmasters but it is not one that should be echoed by writers. In a book published sixty years ago, *The Pleasures of Literature,* John Cowper Powys wrote 'we may have long ago given up "going to church" but few of us with any sensitiveness or curiosity about existence have been able to dodge the familiar scenes and familiar sayings in the Gospels.' This book shows that as far as today's writers are concerned – they (particularly) being people of sensitiveness and curiosity – Jesus is as fascinating a figure as he was to the writers of the past. You can think what you like about him, but you cannot ignore or 'dodge' him – thus confirming his prophecy: 'Heaven and earth shall pass away, but my words shall not pass away.'

I am not sufficiently well read to be able to claim that this selection is at all definitive. But its interest to me, as compiler at least, lies in its unexpectedness. The word anthology derives from the Greek word *anthos* (a flower) and is supposed to represent a garland of pieces of prose or verse. On this occasion I have felt less like someone picking flowers and more like a fisherman casting his net in all kinds of waters and being surprised by the catch, or lack of it. Those authors who one might have expected to have written on the subject say little or nothing, their interest in the human Jesus waning in the same way as Shaw's did in the divine, whereas unlikely characters like Henry Miller, H. L. Mencken and John Updike turn out to have given a great deal of thought to it. This unpredictability has made the job difficult, but more than once I have had the feeling of being guided towards a particular book – picking up Paul Potts in a secondhand bookshop in Newbury or Philip Toynbee in Charing Cross Road, neither writer being at all familiar to me up till then. There seemed to be more than serendipity involved in these chance finds. Sometimes I felt as if Graham Greene, who helped to put the idea in my head originally, was lending a hand – he being the kind of unorthodox Christian who, I feel, would have liked the idea. As far as the living are concerned, I discovered when I was compiling an earlier anthology, *England* (1983), that despite the many promises of help that were made, in the end I had to do the work myself. All the same I would like to thank the faithful few who suggested pieces – especially Paul Foot, John Mortimer, the Revd Mark Mills-Powell, A.N. Wilson and Christopher Silvester. I am also indebted to the late H. Osborne and his book *Whom*

Do Men Say That I Am? (Faber 1932), and also to Teresa Waugh for translating a passage by Rousseau. I would particularly like to thank Deborah Bosley for all her invaluable help in researching and preparing the manuscript.

WHAT WAS HE LIKE?

What's for Supper?

The idea that any man could be speaking for God all the time seems quite inconceivable, even absurd. How much that Jesus said must have been utterly mundane and everyday – e.g. 'I wonder what there'll be for supper?' or 'I'm feeling a bit tired this morning'.

PHILIP TOYNBEE
End of a Journey

Meek and Mild?

The description of 'gentle Jesu, meek and mild' which is commonly provided for our acceptance, does not fit the rather irascible character whom the Evangelists quite frequently portray. 'Forgive your enemies' is a good moral principle, but it is not one to which Jesus is represented as consistently adhering.

A.J. AYER
Thomas Paine

Not Much Hope for the Rest of Us

I saw Martin Scorsese on television discussing *Last Temptation of Christ* saying something to the effect that mankind has concentrated too greatly on the spiritual side of Christ and neglected to appreciate his humanity, but I cannot remember the last time I heard a churchman speaking at length on the numinous aspects of Our Lord. It is ironic that the fundamentalists should have been so vociferous in their protests about *Last Temptation of Christ* since fundamentalism is characterised by a clod-hopping literalness and so is the motivation behind this film. It goes something as follows – Jesus was a man: I am a man: I spend most of my time thinking about sex: ergo, Jesus spent most of his time thinking about sex. The person who wrote the book was clearly a Manichee, for the film is preceded by some lines about his lifelong battle between the flesh and spirit. The point is that the two should, by the Grace of God, co-exist comfortably, not scrap it out in a struggle to the death; and if Jesus didn't get it right then there's very little hope for the rest of us.

ALICE THOMAS ELLIS
Home Life

He Should Have Had a Wife

It is not woman who claims the highest in man. It is a man's own religious soul that drives him on beyond woman, to his supreme activity. For his highest, man is responsible to God alone. He may not pause to remember that he has a life to lose, or a wife and children to leave. He must carry forward the banner of life, though seven worlds perish, with all the wives and mothers and children in them. Hence Jesus, 'Woman, what have I to do with thee?' Every man that lives has to say it again to his wife or mother, once he has any work or mission in hand that comes from his soul.

But again, no man is a blooming marvel for twenty-four hours a day. Jesus or Napoleon or any other of them ought to have been man enough to be able to come home at tea-time and put his slippers on and sit under the spell of his wife. For there you are, the woman has her world, positivity: the world of love, of emotion, of sympathy. And it behooves every man in his hour to take off his shoes and relax and give himself up to his woman and her world. Not to give up his purpose. But to give up himself for a time to her who is his mate. – And so it is one detests the clock-work Kant, and the petit-bourgeois Napoleon divorcing his Josephine for a Hapsburg – or even Jesus, with his 'Woman, what have I to do with thee?' – He might have added 'just now.' – They were all failures.

D.H. LAWRENCE
Fantasia of the Unconscious

A Dignified Bachelor

The mere thought of Jesus as a married man is felt to be blasphemous by the most conventional believers; and even those of us to whom Jesus is not supernatural personage, but a prophet only as Mahomet was a prophet, feel that there was something more dignified in the bachelordom of Jesus than the spectacle of Mahomet lying distracted on the floor of his harem whilst his wives stormed and squabbled and henpecked around him.

GEORGE BERNARD SHAW
Preface to *Androcles and the Lion*

A Shadowy Figure

How shadowy is the figure of Christ as we try to see him in the gospels. What really did he say, what really did he believe, who really was he? Is it better to cling to his loving words and let the others go? – 'the kingdom of heaven is within' . . . 'love one another'. And the best words of all, such words I think as then were spoken for the first time, the words from the cross: 'Father, forgive them, for they know not what they do'. And let the harsh words, and the tyrannical words, and the ambiguous words, go? – e.g., 'No man cometh unto the Father except by me'. And the peculiarly ambiguous words that have always puzzled me, and I daresay a good many other people too, as for instance: 'Render unto Caesar the things that are Caesar's'. Such vile things can be Caesar's as Blake wrote: 'The deadliest poison ever known,/Came from Caesar's laurel crown'. This saying, taken down the ages, would surely have cut at the root of all opposition to tyranny. As again – at the roots of social reform – his words: 'The poor you have always with you'. And the peculiar saying: 'How can you love God whom you have not seen if you cannot love your brother whom you have seen?' But it is because we have seen our brother that it is so difficult to love him.

These words must have meant something else? I dare say, I dare say. If Christ was 'good', they certainly must have meant something else. Again you see the ranks close, and I expect a good many non-Christians and atheists will be found in these ranks, they choose to defend Christ and the belief that Christ is good. And in so far as this closing of the ranks may be seen as the effort of our race to worship Good on the one hand, and on the other hand, to keep their idea of 'Goodness' clothed still in the extraordinary doctrines of the Trinity, the Incarnation, the Redemption of Man by Christ's death upon the cross, is it so commendable? Not very, I think, because the people who make this effort are not docile to truth; they will not follow where the argument leads because if they did they would have to give up these doctrines. This, out of fear, out of love, out of habit, or merely out of an inability to reason, they will not do. Still 'An honest God's the noblest work of man' has in its rather facile cynicism I suppose some truth – yet stops short, I think, of a greater truth. And the greater truth is what I have tried to bring out in this rather long poem, called 'Was He Married?' It is a poem for two voices One voice, the simple, young one, is complaining that Christ could not have known human suffering because human suffering has its roots in imperfection, and he was perfect. The other voice is older, and not very kind.

Was He Married?

Was he married, did he try
To support as he grew less fond of them
Wife and family?

No,
He never suffered such a blow.

Did he feel pointless, feeble and distrait,
Unwanted by everyone and in the way?

From his cradle he was purposeful,
His bent strong and his mind full.

Did he love people very much
Yet find them die one day?

He did not love in the human way.

Did he ask how long it would go on,
Wonder if Death could be counted on for an end?

He did not feel like this,
He had a future of bliss.

Did he never feel strong
Pain for being wrong?

He was not wrong, he was right,
He suffered from others', not his own, spite.

But there is *no* suffering like having made a mistake
Because of being of an inferior make.

He was not inferior,
He was superior.

He knew then that power corrupts but some must govern?

His thoughts were different.

Did he lack friends? Worse,
Think it was for his fault, not theirs?

He did not lack friends,
He had disciples he moulded to his ends.

Did he feel over-handicapped sometimes, yet must draw
    even?

How could he feel like this? He was the King of Heaven.

. . . find a sudden brightness one day in everything
Because a mood had been conquered, or a sin?

I tell you, he did not sin.

Do only human beings suffer from the irritation
I have mentioned, learn too that being comical
Does not ameliorate the desperation?

Only human beings feel this,
It is because they are so mixed.

All human beings should have a medal,
A god cannot carry it, he is not able.

A god is Man's doll, you ass,
He makes him up like this on purpose.

He might have made him up worse.

He often has, in the past.

To choose a god of love, as he did and does,
Is a little move then?

Yes, it is.

A larger one will be made when men
Love love and hate hate but do not deify them?

It will be a larger one.

STEVIE SMITH
Me Again

He Didn't Even Own a Toothbrush

As often as I've read the Gospels I've never run across a single reference to the baggage that Jesus toted around. There is not even mention of a satchel, such as Somerset Maugham made use of when walking about in China. (Bufano, the sculptor, travels lighter than any man I know, but even Bennie is obliged to carry a shaving kit in which he stuffs a change of linen, a toothbrush and a pair of socks.) As for Jesus, by all accounts he didn't even own a toothbrush. No baggage, no furniture, no change of linen, no handkerchief, no passport, no identity card, no bank-book, no love letters, no insurance policy, no address-book. To be sure, he had no wife, no children, no home (not even a winter palace) and no correspondence to look after. As far as we know, he never wrote a line. Home was wherever he happened to be. Not where he hung his hat – because he never wore a hat.

He had no wants, that's the thing. He didn't even have to think about such a menial job as a wardrobe attendant. After a time he ceased working as a carpenter. Not that he was looking for bigger wages. No, he had more important work to do. He set out to prove the absurdity of living by the sweat of one's brow. *Behold the lilies in the field . . .*

HENRY MILLER
Big Sur & The Oranges of Hieronymous Bosch

He Never Nagged

Perhaps it is no wonder that the women were first at the Cradle and last at the Cross. They had never known a man like this Man – there had never been such another. A prophet and teacher who never nagged at them, who never flattered or coaxed or patronized; who never made arch jokes about them, never treated them either as 'The women, God help us!' or 'The ladies, God bless them!'; who rebuked without querulousness and praised without condescension; who took their questions and arguments seriously, who never mapped out their sphere for them, never urged them to be feminine or jeered at them for being female; who had no axe to grind and uneasy male dignity to defend; who took them as he found them and was completely unselfconscious.

There is no act, no sermon, no parable in the whole Gospel that borrows its pungency from female perversity; nobody could possibly guess from the words of Jesus that there was anything 'funny' about woman's nature.

But we might easily deduce it from His contemporaries, and from His prophets before Him, and from His Church to this day.

DOROTHY SAYERS
Are Women Human?

‒‒‒⇁

Jesus and the Children

How we have fixed on this scene! Or did we fix on it before the Victorians fell in love with childhood? It's not, after all, a staple of Renaissance iconography, where the only interesting children were angelic or divine.

He was interested in children in a way that was really original. I look in the Biblical Concordance for references to children in the Old Testament: 'In sorrow bring forth children' . . . 'Give me children or I die' . . . 'The father's children shall bow down' . . . 'Seled died without children' . . . 'The children rebelled against me' . . . 'The children's teeth are set on edge.' Job pleads for the sake of children, but Elisha sends a bear after the boys who made fun of him. Nowhere, though, is there concern for the education, for the upbringing of children, the inner lives of children, the idea that they exist not as possessions, as markers, as earthly immortality, but in themselves. Jesus's concern for them is practical: how do we treat children to help them grow? How do we help children achieve salvation? He seriously thinks of their souls.

Jesus seems genuinely to want the physical presence of children, their company. We often hear Him trying to keep people away, or see Him trying to get away from them, but He rebukes the disciples for shooing children away. He is described in a state of affectionateness. Surely, He is the only affectionate hero in literature. Who can imagine an affectionate Odysseus,

Aeneas? Even a novel would be queasy dwelling too long on a scene like this. Affection – a step, many steps below passion, usually connected to women. He is both maternal and paternal with the children. 'He put his arms around them, laid hands upon them, and blessed them.'

And yet it is exactly this scene, this event, that generates his most harsh dualism. It is in relation to protecting children that He urges His followers to mutilate themselves in the face of temptation that might prove too strong. He puts his hands on the children and then urges His followers to cut off their own hands. He embraces the children and in the next breath tells the rich man that if he will not give up everything he cannot enter the Kingdom of God. He blesses the children and then says, 'There is no one who has given up home, brothers or sisters, mother, father or children ... who will not receive in this age a hundred times as much – houses, brothers, sisters, mothers and children, and land – and persecutions besides; and in the age to come eternal life.'

But of course it is exactly this extremism that makes Jesus not Victorian and therefore not sentimental. Is it possible to have a vision that is at once sentimental and eschatological? This may be the one new contributions of the TV evangelists: the angel with the flaming sword is guarding home and hearth. And, of course, the TV. Usually, though, it is the eschatological that prevents the sentimental; and for that reason, if no other, it is desirable.

He is a complicated character. 'Character' in both senses of the word: literary and colloquial (as in 'He's a real character', implying the capacity for surprising behaviour). Without our knowing it, without our being permitted to articulate it, was the very complexity of Jesus's character, the self-contractions, the progressions forward and backwards, what made Him so compelling, so that even after belief had ceased, we brooded on the figure?

In Jesus, the rejection, always, of the middle ground.

MARY GORDON
Incarnation

So Harsh

28th Feb 1965.

Somewhat better today: have managed to get dressed but can only move with utmost caution. Never know when some apparently innocent movement will bring on a spasm of pain ... I have *no inclination whatever* to write. What is the sensible thing to do? Force myself or deliberately give up? Awful guilt when I do nothing. These states of mind are of course familiar. Any physical illness always demoralizes me terribly. I feel stale, listless, poisoned all through. In these states I really feel as if I could go mad if there were no one else about the place. Simply decline into total inertia. Oh God, help me! ...

It is no good – the Old Testament is absolutely incomprehensible to me for the most part. I do not know *how* we are supposed to understand all these slaughterings and burnt sacrifices. I *can* see the thread running through, the people constantly turning to false gods and God constantly making a new covenant with them.

The New Testament is often of very little comfort. Christ seems so harsh sometimes – to demand the impossible of human nature. One wonders if *anyone* but great saints and ascetics can be saved?

ANTONIA WHITE
Diaries

Not Quite the Tone

There is one very serious defect to my mind in Christ's moral character, and that is that he believed in hell. I do not myself feel that any person who is really profoundly humane can believe in everlasting punishment. Christ certainly as depicted in the Gospels did believe in everlasting punishment, and one does find repeatedly a vindictive fury against those people who would not listen to his preaching – an attitude which is not uncommon with preachers, but which does somewhat detract from superlative excellence. You do not, for instance, find that attitude in Socrates. You find him quite bland and urbane towards the people who would not listen to him; and it is, to my mind, far more worthy of a sage to take that line than to take the line of indignation. You probably all remember the sort of things that Socrates was saying when he was dying, and the sort of things that he generally did say to people who did not agree with him.

You will find that in the Gospels Christ said: 'Ye serpents, ye generations of vipers, how can ye escape the damnation of hell.' That was said to people who did not like his preaching. It is not really to my mind quite the best tone, and there are a great many of these things about hell. There is, of course, the familiar text about sin against the Holy Ghost: 'Whosoever speaketh against the Holy Ghost it shall not forgiven him neither in this world nor in the world to come'. That text has caused an unspeakable amount of misery in the world, for all sorts of people have imagined that they have committed the sin against the Holy Ghost, and thought that it would not be forgiven them either in this world or in the world to come. I really do not think that a person with a proper degree of kindliness in his nature would have put fears and terrors of that sort into the world.

Then Christ says: 'The Son of Man shall send forth His angels, and they shall gather out of His kingdom all things that offend, and them which do iniquity, and shall cast them into a furnace of fire; there shall be wailing and gnashing of teeth'; and he goes on about the wailing and gnashing of teeth. It comes in one verse after another, and it is quite manifest to the reader that there is a certain pleasure in contemplating the wailing and gnashing of teeth, or else it would not occur so often. Then you all, of course, remember about the sheep and the goats: 'Depart from Me, ye cursed, into everlasting fire'. Then he says again: 'If thy hand offend thee, cut if off; it is better for thee to enter into life maimed, than having two hands to go into hell, into the fire that never shall be quenched'. He repeats that again and again also. I must say that I think that all this doctrine, that hell fire is a punishment for sin, is a doctrine of cruelty. It is a doctrine that put cruelty into the world and gave the world generations of cruel torture; and the Christ of the Gospels, if you could take him as his chroniclers represent him, would certainly have to be considered partly responsible for that.

There are other things of less importance. There is the instance of the Gadarene swine, where it certainly was not very kind to the pigs to put the devils into them and make them rush down the hill to the sea. You must remember that he was omnipotent, and he could have made the devils simply go away; but he chooses to send them into the pigs. Then there is the curious story of the fig-tree, which always rather puzzled me. You remember what happened about the fig-tree. 'He was hungry; and seeing a fig-tree afar off having leaves, He came if haply He might find anything thereon; and He came to it He found nothing but leaves, for the time of figs was not yet. And Jesus answered and said unto it: "No man eat fruit of thee hereafter for ever"; . . . and Peter saith unto him: "Master, behold the fig-tree which thou cursedst is withered away".' That is a very curious story, because it was not the right time of year for figs, and you really could not blame the tree. I cannot myself feel that either in the matter of wisdom or in the matter of virtue Christ stands quite as high as some people known to history. I think I should put Buddha and Socrates above him in those respects.

BERTRAND RUSSELL
Why I Am Not a Christian

A Jewish Radical

He thinks like a Jew. He talks like a Jew. And he was betrayed by the Jewish establishment. Nothing new there.

NORMAN MAILER
Waterstones Magazine

A Jew by Birth

I know a good Christian of Hamburg who could never suppress his discontent at the fact that our Lord and Saviour was a Jew by birth. A deep fit of ill-humour seized hold of him every time when forced to confess that the Man who was a model of perfection and deserved the greatest veneration, yet belonged to the race of those pockethandkerchiefless, long-nosed Jews whom he saw hawking as pedlars about the streets, and whom he so heartily hated; and who were yet more fatal to him when they took to high commerce and dealt in spices and logwood and so interfered with his own interests.

HEINRICH HEINE
Shakespeare's Maids and Women

A Distorted Personality

All four [Gospels] agree in giving us a picture of a very definite personality; they carry the same conviction of reality that the early accounts of Buddha do. In spite of miraculous and incredible additions, one is obliged to say, 'Here was a man. This part of the tale could not have been invented'.

But just as the personality of Gautama Buddha has been distorted and obscured by the stiff squatting figure, the gilded idol of later Buddhism, so one feels that the lean and strenuous personality of Jesus is much wronged by the unreality and conventionality that a mistaken reverence has imposed upon his figure in modern Christian art. Jesus was a penniless teacher, who wandered about the dusty sun-bit country of Judea, living upon casual gifts of food; yet he is always represented clean, combed and sleek, in spotless raiment, erect, and with something motionless about him as though he was gliding through the air. This alone has made him unreal and incredible to many people who cannot distinguish the core of the story from the ornamental and unwise additions of the unintelligently devout.

And it may be that the early parts of the gospels are accretions of the same nature. The miraculous circumstances of the birth of Jesus, the great star that brought wise men from the east to worship at his manger cradle, the massacre of the male infant children in the region of Bethlehem by Herod as a consequence of these portents, and the flight into Egypt, are all supposed to be such accretionary matter by many authorities. At the best they are events unnecessary to the teaching, and rob it of much of the strength and power it possesses when we strip it of such accompaniment . . .

We are left, if we do strip this record of these difficult accessories, with the figure of a being, very human, very earnest and passionate, capable of swift anger, and teaching a new and simple and profound doctrine – namely, the universal loving Fatherhood of God and the coming of the Kingdom of Heaven. He is clearly a person – to use a common phrase – of intense personal magnetism. He attracted followers and filled them with love and courage. Weak and ailing people were heartened and healed by his presence. Yet he was probably of delicate physique, because of the swiftness of which he died under the pains of crucifixion. There is a tradition that he fainted when, according to the custom, he was made to bear his cross the place of execution. When he first appeared as a teacher he was a man of about thirty. He went about the country for three years spreading his doctrine, and then he came to Jerusalem and was accused of trying to set up a strange kingdom in Judea; he was tried upon this charge, and crucified together with two thieves. Long before they were dead, his sufferings were over.

H.G. WELLS
A Short History of the World

Jesus Was Illiterate

Christ and his Apostles were Illiterate Men: Caiaphas, Pilate & Herod were learned . . .

WILLIAM BLAKE
Annotations on Dr Thornton's Translation of the Lord's Prayer

'No Time Ago'

no time ago
or else a life
walking in the dark
i met christ

jesus)my heart
flopped over
and lay still
while he passed(as

close as i'm to you
yes closer
made of nothing
except loneliness

E.E CUMMINGS
XAIPE

≁

Rejecting the Nativity

My solution to the problem of Jesus's nativity implies a rejection of the mystical Virgin Birth doctrine and will therefore offend many otherwise irreligious Christians, even though the doctrine cannot be traced earlier than the second century A.D. and cannot be reconciled either with *Romans* i. 3, *Hebrews* vii. 14 or *Galatians* iv. 4 – documents which are earlier in date than any of the Canonical Gospels. Its value as a means of asserting the divinity of Jesus and glorifying him equally with heathen gods was first remarked upon by Justin Martyr in his philosophical *Apology for the Christians* (A.D. 139); and its value in exculpating the earlier Christians from any suspicion of trying to revive the Davidic dynasty is clear from the persecutions of the House of David under the Emperors Trajan and Domitian. But the Christians were not wilful liars, and the bold theory of Jesus's miraculous birth could never have been advanced had there not already been a mystery connected with his parentage: it must have seemed the only way of harmonizing the apparently contradictory traditions that Joseph was not Jesus's father though contracted in marriage to Mary (*Matthew* i. 18-19) and that Jesus was 'born under the law' – that is, legitimately – 'that he might redeem those who were under the Law' (*Galatians* iv. 5).

No store should be set by the earliest extant text of *Matthew* i. 16, discovered only recently, according to which 'Joseph begat Jesus'. I take it for an Ebionite interpolation designed to champion Jesus's legitimacy against enemies of Christianity who, like the Roman Celsus, falsely described him as the bastard son of a Greek soldier. The Ebionites' difficulty was that if Mary had already been contracted in marriage to Joseph when he found her pregnant, this would in Jewish Law (*Deuteronomy* xxii. 13-21) have bastardized her child even if the marriage had not been consummated and she had in the interval secretly married someone else. But the solution is infelicitous as contradicting the credible account of Joseph's embarrassment given two verses later in the canonical text and as making nonsense of the story of the interview with Pilate. On the other hand, the Virgin Birth doctrine, now that no one believes the God Hermes to be the Word of Zeus, and Hercules and Dionysus to be his sons, no longer has the same force in religious polemics as it had in Justin's day; and since the prevailing view in Protestant countries is that Jesus was, beyond everything, a moral exemplar, the suggestion that he was not a man in the ordinary sense of the word, and not therefore subject to human error, may be said to discourage imitation of his virtues. True, many saints have held the doctrine serenely, and it can be argued on their behalf that if Jesus is regarded as a mere man his authority is greatly diminished; but to the mass of people nowadays the choice is between a Jesus born in the ordinary course of nature and one as mythical as Perseus or Prometheus.

ROBERT GRAVES
King Jesus

That Scarcely Visible Young Man

I am not saying that Jesus was merely a very good man who said some very wise things; I am saying that Jesus was filled with God, and that in most of what he said and did and suffered he was speaking and acting directly under inspiration.

You will have caught the slightly jarring note of that 'most of'. I do not know how closely the Jesus of the New Testament resembles the man who died at least forty years before the first gospel was written. But I do know that the man who is presented to us in the gospels is the only Jesus we have; and I do know that this man is a humanly contradictory figure who sometimes failed to live up to his own highest teaching. The man who warned us against judging others continually judged the scribes and pharisees with virulent anger: the man who told us to love our enemies sometimes condemned those who refused to accept him to burn everlastingly in hell.

It is an irony of the New Testament that not even Jesus himself could always keep the new and high law which he had given to mankind. And if Jesus was guilty of all-too-human anger how much harder has it been for his followers to love as their master taught them to love. The history of Christianity has been largely a history of their failures.

PHILIP TOYNBEE
Part of a Journey

Our Lord Was a Working Class Person

Our Lord and Socrates, probably the two greatest men yet to live, certainly outside China and India, never wrote anything at all, they just talked; but what talk!

In the whole of recorded history, there is ultimately no proof that there is a God and equally, however, there is positively no proof that there is not one. Those who believe in authority tend to believe in God, those who love equality, not to. There are exceptions to this, there are exceptions to everything.

To me the only possible explanation, not only of Our Lord's life, but also of his fame, is to admit that he was the supreme artist of human goodness. He was to goodness what Shakespeare was to language, Spinoza to thought, Rembrandt to painting and Beethoven to music. He is more loved in Italy than Dante, and in France than wine. This takes some doing when one remembers the dreadful things done in his name.

One thing that is certain is that he was very Hebrew. Galilee was the Provence of the Hebrew world. And although he was probably more like St Francis than he was Spinoza, no one will really understand Our Lord who does not know a lot about the Jews.

He was very attractive to women. At least there were always a lot of women about.

Perhaps he never did actually raise the dead, but he made the living very happy, especially at the marriage feast of Cana. Perhaps he did not actually change the water into wine, but nobody, not even St Paul, ever accused him of stopping people having a drink.

He was drunk with the Old Testament. The Isaiah, who wrote before the Babylonian Captivity did in fact prophesy his coming in the very factual sense, that he was terribly like him. Although he was an aristocrat and Our Lord was a working-class person. Our Lord dropped his aitches.

Nobody knows what he looked like. But what we do know is that he definitely did not look a bit like any painting or sculpture we have of him. Even when they are the work of really great artists, artists as great as Fra Angelico, Donatello or El Greco. Because he was an Asian working-class person, a Jewish prophet not a christian knight. He wasn't even a

European let alone a christian. The nearest people in appearance, who are alive today, to Our Lord and his family and friends in the New Testament, are the Yemenite Jews in Israel. Of all the thousands of portraits of him by christian artists throughout the centuries, not one of them ever thought of making him look like a working man, let alone a Jew.

Our Lord was very young; when he got fed up with grownups he used to go and play with the kids. He loved women, he was always on their side against men. And as to his own relations with a girl, he said 'There are those who have turned themselves into eunuchs for the Kingdom of Heaven's sake'. And the Kingdom of Heaven meant the Commonwealth of Man. Yet his name has become a swear word and a curse and who is to blame for that?

PAUL POTTS
Dante Called You Beatrice

Thomas Carlyle's Vision

It was Carlyle's second visit to my studio that best revealed the inner nature of the man, when 'The Awakened Conscience' and 'The Light of the World' were just completed. He spoke approvingly of the first, but without any artistic understanding of the effect, he pointed to the reflection of the green foliage into the shining table and said, 'The moonlight is well given'; turning to the other, he spoke in terms of disdain. 'You call that thing, I ween, a picture of Jesus Christ. Now you cannot gain any profit to yourself except in mere pecuniary sense, or profit any one else on earth, in putting into a shape a mere papistical fantasy like that, for it can only be an inanity, or a delusion to every one that may look on it. It is a poor mistaken presentation of the noblest, the brotherliest, and the most heroic-minded Being that every walked God's earth. Do you ever suppose that Jesus walked about bedizened in priestly robes and a crown, and with yon jewels on His breast, and a gilt aureole round His head? Ne'er crown nor pontifical robe did the world e'er give to such as He. Well – and if you mean to represent Him as the spiritual Christ, you have chosen the form in which he has been travestied from the beginning by world-lings who have recorded their own ambitions as His, repeating Judas' betrayal to the high priests. You should think frankly of His antique heroic soul; if you realised his character at all you wouldn't try to make people go back and worship the image that priests have invented of Him, to keep men's silly souls in meshes of slavery and darkness. Don't you see that you're help-ing to make people believe what you know to be false, what ye don't believe yourself? The picture I was looking at just now of the shallow, idle fool and his wretched victim had to do with reality; this is only empty make-believe, mere pretended fancy, to do the like of which is the worst of occupations for a man to take to'. I tried to declare that I did firmly believe in the idea that I had painted, more than anything I saw with my natural eyes, and that I could prove from his writings that he did also – here he raised his voice well-nigh to a scream, and Mrs. Carlyle standing behind, put up her emphatic finger and shook her head, signing to me.

He vouchsafed but passing notice of my defence. 'It's a' wilful blindness, ye persuade yourself that ye do believe, but it's high time that ye gave up the habit of deluding yourself'. I tried again to say that his own teaching was of the spirit of truth coming to men, who are bound to listen, and that no Spirit of Truth was so candid as that which Christ represents; but he would not stop, and his good wife more vehemently beckoned silence. 'I'll tell ye what my interest in the matter is', he said; 'I have a screen at home, and on it I have put portraits, the best I can anyhow get – often enough I have to be content with very poor ones – of all the men that ever were on earth who have helped to make us something better than wild beasts of rapine and havoc; of all the bravehearted creatures whose deeds and words have made life a term of years to bear with patience and faith, and I see what manner of men most of these were; Socrates and Plato, Alexander, Pompey, Caesar, aye, and Brutus, and many another man of the old time who won or lost in the struggle to do what they deemed the justest and wisest thing. By the help of these effigies I can conjure each up to my eyes as though the ancients were old acquaintances, and I can call up more or less vividly many a man of the time that has come since; but that grandest of all beings, that Jesus of heavenly omens, I have no means whatever of raising up to my sight with any accredited form'. Taking a long breath here, he proceeded as if to a new chapter: 'I am only a poor man, but I can say in serious truth that I'd thankfully give one third of all the little store of money saved for my wife and old age, for a veritable contemporary image of Jesus Christ, showing Him as He walked about, as He was trying with His ever invincible soul to break down the obtuse stupidity of the cormorant-minded, bloated gang who were doing, in desperate contention, their utmost to make the world go devilward with themselves. Search has been made honestly, and imposture has striven to satisfy the desire to procure some portraits of Him, but not the faintest shadow exists that can be accepted, nor any legendic attempt to represent Him can be credited, notwithstanding your fables of King Abgarus of Edessa or of St Luke or of St Veronica's napkin. Yet there were artists enough and to spare, and the sculptors' work has come down to us, filling all the museums of Europe. They adored their stone images of obsolete gods, and looked to the augurs of these as ruling their destinies, while the living mouthpiece of God, the giver of true wisdom, was amongst them. It was a shadow-land in which they searched for their gods, and so made images of Jupiter, of Apollo, of Hercules, of all the deities and deesses who put no bridle upon the will of their votaries, but left them to play into the hands of all the devils in hell, from whose reign indeed they were not separated, unless forsooth we have to take them for creatures of purposeless fancy. Male and female, they were the rulers of a heaven that all the intelligent among men had long ceased to believe in, spite of the statue of the ''Son of Man'', as he called Himself, and shown us what manner of man He was, what his height, what His build, and what the features of His sorrow-marked face were, and what His dress, I for one would have thanked him who did it with all the gratitude of my heart for that portrait, as the most precious heirloom of the ages. Now I tell you, young man, you are doing exactly what the sculptors of Roman time did, and y'll ne'er make your talent a benefit to your fellowmen of to-day and to them that come afterwards, if you go on working at worn-out fables. I have seen the pictures, all of them by the great painters who have set themselves to portray Jesus, and what could be more wide o' of the mark? There's the picture of ''Christ Disputing with the Doctors'' in our National Gallery by Leonardo da Vinci, and it makes him a puir, weak, girl-faced nonentity, bedecked in a fine silken sort of gown, with gems and precious stones bordering the whole, just as though He had been the darling of a Court, with hands and fingers that have never done any work, and could do none whatever, a creature indeed altogether incapable of convincing any novice advanced enough to solve the simplest problem in logic. There are other notable presentations of conceptions of Christ in paint and marble familiar to us in prints, and they are all alike'. Here in shrill voice and high, he continued, 'And when I look, I say, ''Thank you, Mr da Vinci'', ''Thank you, Mr Michael Angelo'', ''Thank you Mr Raffaelle'', that may be your idea of Jesus Christ, but I've another of my own which I very much prefer." I see the Man toiling along in the hot sun, at times in the cold wind, going long stages, tired, hungry often and footsore, drinking at the spring, eating by the way, His rough and patched clothes bedraggled and covered with dust, imparting blessings to others which no human power, be it king's or emperor's or priest's, was strong enough to give to Him, a missioner of Heaven sent with brave tongue to utter doom on the babbling world and its godless nonsense, and to fashion out another teaching to supplant it, doing battle with that valiant voice of His, only against the proud and perverse, and charming the simple by His love and lovableness, but ever disencharming such as would suppose that the kingdom of heaven that He preached would bring to Him or to His adherents earthly glory or riches; offering them rather ignominy and death. Surrounded by His little band of almost unteachable poor friends, I see Him dispirited, dejected, and at times broken down in hope by the immovability and spleen of fools, who, being rich with armed slaves, determined to make the heavens bend to them. I see Him unflinching in faith and spirit crying out, "He that hath ears to hear let him hear". This was a man worth seeing the likeness of, if such could be found. One painter indeed there was who had some gleam of penetration in him, and faculty of representation, and his works I look for wherever I can hope to find them. Albert Durer is that man, who illustrated the painful story of the Christ, the Man of Sorrows, in His babyhood nursed amid ruins, with Joseph ever toiling, and the Mother oppressed and haggard with thought, and the child without the carelessness and joy of infancy, being lean and prematurely sad, and then step after step of the same heavy burdened soul appears, until, with face worn and distorted, He ends His life of misery upon the Cross; but even Albert Durer had canons of tradition which hindered him from giving the full truth, and I don't see what he failed to do then. Take my word for it, and use your cunning hand and eyes for something that ye see about ye, like the fields and trees I saw here a year ago, and, above all, do not confuse your understanding with mysteries' . . .

HOLMAN HUNT

Pre-Raphaelitism and the Pre-Raphaelite Brotherhood

No Billy Graham

If Christ had been as successful as Billy Graham, we should never have heard of him.

MALCOLM MUGGERIDGE

quoted in I. Hunter, *Malcolm Muggeridge: A Life*

The Face in the Mirror

The only way in which we can possibly visualise Christ and the Devil is the same, by looking in the mirror.

W.H. AUDEN

quoted in R. Davenport-Hines, *Auden*

He Would Have Been Locked Up

If the Lunatic Asylum as at present established had existed three thousand years ago, we may or may not have had Greece and Rome – it is doubtful – but we should certainly have had no Old Testament and no New. The Hebrew religion would have perished of anaemia and the Christian religion could never have been born. Nearly all the prophets of the Jews from Samuel on are patients for the alienists and candidates for the Asylum. Had there been a Lunatic Asylum in the suburbs of Jerusalem, Jesus Christ would infallibly have been shut up in it at the outset of his public career. That interview with Satan on a pinnacle of the Temple would alone have damned him, and everything that happened after could but have confirmed the diagnosis. The whole religious complexion of the modern world is due to the absence from Jerusalem of a Lunatic Asylum.

HAVELOCK ELLIS
Impressions & Comments

A Doctor Writes

We know nothing about the physical appearance of Jesus or the state of his health.

ALBERT SCHWEITZER
The Psychiatric Study of Jesus

The Finest of All Documents

I am unable to believe that God exists or that either Christ or Mahommed was his prophet. I consider that the Christian doctrine is the most perfect yet devised and I reverence Christ as a man of almost super-human sympathy, courage, pathos and spiritual beauty: but I do not find it possible, or necessary, to attribute to him divine attributes.

To me, the New Testament is the finest of all human documents, but even as a boy I failed entirely to understand why the Old Testament should be regarded as anything more than a harsh tribal history.

HAROLD NICOLSON
My Philosophy of Life: A Symposium

A Character of Wild Contradictions

It seems quite impossible for us now to do as the old-fashioned rationalists used to do and deny roundly that Jesus ever existed. The personality of the man, as St Luke at any rate describes it,

has the unmistakable mark of a Real human character: but it is
a character full of wild contradictions, beautiful, bewildering,
heart-breaking and rather frightening, and so much the opposite
of that 'sweet reasonableness' Matthew Arnold absurdly attributes to it, that it is hard to say in any detail what you would
have to do if you came under its spell.

JOHN COWPER POWYS
The Pleasures of Literature

—↗—

Oddly Petulant

There's this brave, witty, sometimes oddly petulant, man strid-
ing around in an occupied territory knowing and then not wanting to know that he's bound to die and to die painfully. And
in the middle of it all, to say things that have never been said,
and are still not said, about love. As a model of what human
behaviour can be like, it still stands supreme.

DENNIS POTTER
quoted in H. Carpenter, *Dennis Potter: A Life*

—↗—

A Supreme Individualist

And above all, Christ is the most supreme of individualists.
Humility, like the artistic acceptance of all experiences, is merely
a mode of manifestation. It is man's soul that Christ is always
looking for. He calls it 'God's Kingdom' and finds it in everyone.
He compares it to little things, to a tiny seed, to a handful of
leaven, to a pearl. That is because one realises one's soul only
by getting rid of all alien passions, all acquired culture, and all
external possessions, be they good or evil.

I bore up against everything with some stubbornness of will
and much rebellion of nature, till I had absolutely nothing left
in the world but one thing. I had lost my name, my position,

my happiness, my freedom, my wealth. I was a prisoner and a pauper. But I still had my children left. Suddenly they were taken away from me by the law. It was a blow so appalling that I did not know what to do, so I flung myself on my knees, and bowed my head, and wept, and said, 'The body of a child is as the body of the Lord: I am not worthy of either'. That moment seemed to save me. I saw then that the only thing for me was to accept everything. Since then – curious as it will no doubt sound – I have been happier. It was of course my soul in its ultimate essence that I had reached. In many ways I had been its enemy, but I found it waiting for me as a friend. When one comes in contact with the soul it makes one simple as a child, as Christ said one should be.

It is tragic how few people ever 'possess their souls' before they die. 'Nothing is more rare in any man,' says Emerson, 'than an act of his own.' It is quite true. Most people are other people. Their thoughts are someone else's opinions, their lives a mimicry, their passions a quotation. Christ was not merely the supreme individualist, but he was the first individualist in history. People have tried to make him out an ordinary philanthropist, or ranked him as an altruist with the unscientific and sentimental. But he was really neither one nor the other. Pity he has, of course, for the poor, for those who are shut up in prisons, for the lowly, the wretched; but he has far more pity for the rich, for the hard hedonists, for those who waste their freedom in becoming slaves to things, for those who wear soft raiment and live in king's houses. Riches and pleasures seemed to him to be really greater tragedies than poverty or sorrow. And as for altruism, who knew better than he that it is vocation not volition that determines us, and that one cannot gather grapes of thorns or figs from thistles?

To live for others as a definite self-conscious aim was not the basis of his creed. When he says, 'Forgive your enemies' it is not for the sake of the enemy, but for one's own sake that he says so, and because love is more beautiful than hate. In his own entreaty to the young man, 'Sell all that thou hast and give to the poor', it is not of the state of the poor that he is thinking, but of the soul of the young man, the soul that wealth was marring. In his view of life he is one with the artist who knows that by the inevitable law of self-perfection, the poet must sign, and sculptor think in bronze, and the painter make the world a mirror for his moods, as surely and as certainly as the hawthorn must blossom in spring, and the corn turn to gold at harvest-time, and the moon in her ordered wanderings change from shield to sickle and from sickle to shield.

To the artist, expression is the only mode under which he can conceive life at all. To him what is dumb is dead. But to Christ it was not so. With a width and wonder of imagination that fills one almost with awe, he took the entire world of the inarticulate, voiceless world of pain, as his kingdom, and made of himself its eternal mouthpiece. Those of whom I have spoken, who are dumb under oppression and 'whose silence is heard only of God', he chose as his brothers. He sought to become eyes to the blind, ears to the deaf, and a cry in the lips of those whose tongues had been tied. His desire was to be to the myriads who had found no utterance a very trumpet through which they might call to heaven. And feeling, with the artistic nature of one to whom suffering and sorrow were modes through which he could realise his conception of the beautiful, that an idea is of no value till it becomes incarnate and is made an image, he made of himself the image of the Man of Sorrows, and as such has fascinated and dominated art as no Greek god ever succeeded in doing.

OSCAR WILDE
De Profundis

So Few Knew Him

The more I think about Jesus of Nazareth the more heart-breaking it seems that so very few people were able to know him. All we have of his ministry is a jumble of corrupted words: but he himself must have been so much more wonderful than even the best of his words.

PHILIP TOYNBEE
End of a Journey

HOW HAVE WE
TAMED HIM?

I Come Not to Bring Peace

I will admit that one prediction of Jesus Christ has been indisputably fulfilled: *I come not to bring peace upon earth but a sword.*

PERCY BYSSHE SHELLEY

Shelley's Prose

I See His Splendour

The greater part of Men make their way with the same instinctiveness, the same unwandering eye from their purposes, the same animal eagerness as the Hawk. The Hawk wants a Mate, so does the Man – look at them both they set about it and procure one in the same manner. They want both a nest and they both set about one in the same manner – they get their food in the same manner – The noble animal Man for his amusement smokes his pipe – the Hawk balances about the clouds – that is the only difference of their leisures. This it is that makes the Amusement of Life – to a speculative Mind. I go among the Fields and catch a glimpse of a Stoat or a fieldmouse peeping out of the withered grass – the creature hath a purpose and its eyes are bright with it. I go amongst the buildings of a city and

I see a Man hurrying along – to what? The Creature has a purpose and his eyes are bright with it. But then, as Wordsworth says, 'we have all one human heart' – there is an electric fire in human nature tending to purify – so that among these human creatures there is continually some birth of new heroism. The pity is that we must wonder at it: as we should at finding a pearl in rubbish. I have no doubt that thousands of people never heard of have had hearts completely disinterested: I can remember but two – Socrates and Jesus – their Histories evince it. What I heard a little time ago, Taylor observe with respect to Socrates may be said of Jesus – That he was so great a man that though he transmitted no writing of his own to posterity, we have his Mind and his sayings and his greatness handed to us by others. It is to be lamented that the history of the latter was written and revised by Men interested in the pious frauds of Religion. Yet through all this I see his splendour.

JOHN KEATS
Letters of John Keats

No Place to Lay His Head

I prefer the man I meet in the Gospels, to the God described in the work of theologians. It is a great pity, a very foolish thing, to allow either a bishop or an atheist to steal him away from us. And don't let a committee or a commissar turn you against freedom.

They are awful cheats these christians, for nearly 2,000 years the story of Barabbas has been a symbol that the world prefers a bad man to a good one. Now Barabbas, whose name was also Jesus, was a leader of the Jewish resistance movement fighting for home rule against the Roman Empire. The crowd then chose one kind of good man against another kind of good man. A kind, that given the circumstances of the time, was easier for them to understand.

Throughout history man has had the talent to choose the best of his own king, Our Lord and Socrates, and then they change them to their likeness. But there is hope in the fact that they do choose them. Even St Paul and Plato chose Our Lord and Socrates and not themselves.

More buildings have been built in his honour than there are in all London. If all the Gothic cathedrals and Byzantine basilicas, all the Benedictine monasteries and Carthusian abbeys, all the Anglican churches and Methodist chapels, all the convents and schools and all the Vaticans and St Sophias, all the Latin shrines and Protestant missions, all the Carmelite priories and Dominican convents, all the Roman, Anglican, Orthodox, Coptic, Marionite, Ethiopian, Syrian, Baptist, Quaker, Non-Conformist and Armenian places of worship were brought together in one place, New York and Moscow would appear as small cities and Dublin and Venice as villages. Yet while he was alive he very often had no place to lay his head.

PAUL POTTS
Dante Called You Beatrice

Could Christ Have Sinned?

Again and again as I twisted and turned myself, in quite as much of a twisting and turning as our friends' today in the Christian churches, I found, or so it seemed to me, the tangles and entanglements to be of Christianity's own making: as to these two points especially, which still today, grown up and grown old as I am, puzzle me. The first is the doctrine of the Redemption, this Bargain, this really monstrous Bargain, that God would save his little children, once so loved and favoured and now gone hopelessly astray, only by the death of his son, the Second Person of the Trinity, co-equal and co-eternal, upon the cross in man's form and nature. This seems a Bargain dishonourable both to proposer and accepter, and productive of great harm to the human race because of the burden of guilt and gratitude it imposes, but this is by the way, it is the nature of the Bargain one finds immoral. Once again one thinks of Epicurus: 'Omnipotence could, benevolence could, have found some other way'.

The other point that puzzles me, and to which, though I have often asked, I have found no answer, is the Christian teaching as to the dual nature of Christ – that he was at the same time perfect Man and perfect God. For if he was perfect God, the Second Person of the Trinity, then he could not sin, because if he had sinned the Trinity would have sinned too, and this is not possible, for the Trinity is by definition Perfection, and perfection cannot be less than perfection. But if Christ could not sin, how then was he Man? For Man, even in Christianity's Garden of Eden, had power to sin.

I remember once asking a Roman Catholic friend of mine, an instructor in theology at a famous Benedictine school: Could Christ have sinned? He was horrified, and said: Of course not. And, given the premises of Christian doctrine, he was right, was he not, both to say 'no' and to be horrified.

I found this doctrine of the dual nature of Christ full of the most extreme difficulties and contradictions, and still do, and I wrote this poem about the difficulties. You may think it is curious to write poems so much on argumentative subjects – but so did the Arians, you know, when they rushed about Alexandria, singing their popular song: 'There was a time when the Son was not' – what was this but a poem? My poem is called:

Oh Christianity, Christianity

Oh Christianity, Christianity,

Why do you not answer our difficulties?
If He was God He was not like us,
He could not lose.

Can Perfection be less than perfection?
Can the creator of the Devil be bested by Him?
What can the temptation to possess the earth have meant to
    Him
Who made and possessed it? What do you mean?

And Sin, how could He take our sins upon Him? What does
    it mean?
To take sin upon one is not the same
As to have sin inside one and feel guilty.

It is horrible to feel guilty,
We feel guilty because we are.
Was He horrible? Did He feel guilty?

You say he was born humble – but He was not,
He was born God –
Taking our nature upon Him. But then you say,
He was Perfect Man. Do you mean
Perfectly Man, meaning wholly; or Man without sin? Ah
Perfect Man without sin is not what we are.

Do you mean He did not know that He was God,
Did not know He was the Second Person of the Trinity?
(Oh, if He knew this, and was,
It was a source of strength for Him we do not have)
But this theology of 'emptying' you preach sometimes–
That He emptied Himself of knowing He was God – seems
A theology of false appearances

To mock your facts, as He was God, whether He knew He
   was or not.

Oh what do you mean, what do you mean?
You never answer our difficulties

You say, Christianity, you say
That the Trinity is unchanging from eternity,
But then you say
At the incarnation He took
Out Manhood into the Godhead,
That did not have it before,
So it must have altered it,
Having it.

Oh what do you mean, what do you mean?
You never answer our questions.

But what a tangle they have got themselves into. I do not know
whether one prefers the mental and spiritual gymnastics of the
Catholics, who, aware of the tangle, seek a 'logical' way out,
and when this logic of theirs delivers them into the sort of
impasse I have indicated, reply: 'Well, you must remember we
have been discussing some of the deepest mysteries of our
faith'; implying that there may come a time when what is palpably unreasonable has to be kicked upstairs and called a 'mystery', something that the mere human mind cannot grasp,
'God's reason', et cetera. Or whether one prefers the more usual
Anglican approach which is (or has been, in my experience)
to leave ends dangling and hope for the best – 'Well, we
don't really *know*, do we?' Well, no, of course, I don't really
think we do. But I cannot say this in the sense they do, that
is: I do not think I could say this and retain a belief in the

Christian doctrines of the Trinity, the Incarnation and eternal Hell.

STEVIE SMITH
Me Again

Glorious Martyrdom

A book is put into our hands when children, called the Bible, the purpose of whose history is briefly this: that God made the earth in six days, and there planted a delightful garden, in which he placed the first pair of human beings; [that] in the midst of the garden he planted a tree whose fruit, although within their reach, they were forbidden to touch; that the Devil in the shape of a snake persuaded them to eat of this fruit; in consequence of which God condemned both them and their posterity yet unborn to satisfy his justice by their eternal misery; that, four thousand years after these events (the human race in the meanwhile having gone unredeemed to perdition), God engendered with the betrothed wife of a carpenter in Judea (whose virginity was nevertheless uninjured), and begat a Son, whose name was Jesus Christ; and who was crucified and died, in order that no more men might be devoted to hell-fire, he bearing the burden of his Father's displeasure by proxy. The book states, in addition, that the soul of whoever disbelieves this sacrifice will be burned with everlasting fire.

During many ages of misery and darkness this story gained implicit belief; but at length men arose who suspected that it was a fable and imposture, and that Jesus Christ, so far from being a God, was only a man like themselves. But a numerous set of men who derived and still derive emoluments from this opinion in the shape of a popular belief told the vulgar that if they did not believe in the Bible, they would be damned to all eternity – and burned, imprisoned and poisoned all the unbi-assed and unconnected inquirers who occasionally arose. They still oppress them so far as the people – now become more enlightened – will allow.

The belief in all that the Bible contains is called Christianity. A Roman governor of Judea at the instance of a priest-led mob crucified a man called Jesus eighteen centuries ago. He was a man of pure life, who desired to rescue his countrymen from the tyranny of their barbarous and degrading superstitions. The common fate of all who desire to benefit mankind awaited him. The rabble at the instigation of the priests demanded his death, although his very judgement made public acknowledgment of his innocence. Jesus was sacrificed to the honour of that God with whom he was afterwards confounded. It is of importance, therefore, to distinguish between the pretended character of this being as the Son of God and the Saviour of the world and his real character as a man who for a vain attempt to reform the world paid the forfeit of his life to that overbearing tyranny which has since so long desolated the universe in his name. While the one is a hypocritical demon, who announced himself as the God of compassion and peace even while he stretches forth his blood-red hand with the sword of discord to waste the earth, having confessedly devised this scheme of desolation from eternity; the other stands in the foremost list of those true heroes who have died in the glorious martyrdom of liberty and have braved torture, contempt, and poverty in the cause of suffering humanity.

The vulgar, even in extremes, became persuaded that the crucifixion of Jesus was a supernatural event. Testimonies of miracles, so frequent in unenlightened ages, were not wanting to prove that he was something divine. The belief rolling through the lapse of ages, met with the reveries of Plato and the reasonings of Aristotle and acquired force and extent until the divinity of Jesus became a dogma which to dispute was death, which to doubt was infamy.

PERCY BYSSHE SHELLEY
Shelley's Prose

A Special Attitude Towards Life

The religion of Jesus was the invention of a race which itself never accepted that religion. In the East religions spring up, for the most part, as naturally as flowers, and, like flowers, are scarcely a matter for furious propaganda. These deep sagacious Eastern men threw us of old this rejected flower, as they have since sent us the vases and fans they found too tawdry; and when we send our missionaries out to barter back the gift at a profit, they say no word, but their faces wear the mysterious Eastern smile. Yet for us, at all events, the figure of Jesus symbolises, and will always symbolise, a special attitude towards life, made up of tender human sympathy and mystical reliance on the unseen forces of the world. In certain stories of the Gospels, certain sayings, in many of the parables, this attitude finds the completest expression of its sweetest abandonment. But to us, men of another race living in far distant corners of the world, it seems almost oriental and ascetic, a morbid exceptional phenomenon.

HAVELOCK ELLIS
Affirmations

Something Long Forgotten

To Elsie Moll
New York
Sunday Evening (May 3, 1909)

My Dearest:
[. . .] – To-day I have been roaming about town. In the morning
I walked down-town – stopping once to watch three flocks of
pigeons circling in the sky. I dropped into St John's chapel an
hour before the service and sat in the last pew and looked
around. It happens that last night at the Library I read a life of
Jesus and I was interested to see what symbols of that life
appeared in the chapel. I think there were none at all excepting
the gold cross on the altar. When you compare that poverty
with the wealth of symbols, of remembrances, that were created
and revered in times past, you appreciate the change that has
come over the church. The church should be more than a moral
institution, if it is to have the influence that it should have. The
space, the gloom, the quiet mystify and entrance the spirit. But
that is not enough. – And one turns from this chapel to those
built by men who felt the wonder of the life and death of Jesus
– temples full of sacred images, full of the air of love and
holiness – tabernacles hallowed by worship that sprang from
the noble depths of men familiar with Gethsemane, familiar
with Jerusalem. – I do not wonder that the church is so largely
a relic. Its vitality depended on its association with Palestine,
so to speak. – I felt a peculiar emotion in reading about John
the Baptist, Bethany, Galilee – and so on, because (the truth is)
I had not thought about them much since my days at Sunday-
school (when, of course, I didn't think about them at all.) It was
like suddenly remembering something long-forgotten, or else
like suddenly seeing something new and strange in what had
always been in my mind. – Reading the life of Jesus, too, makes

one distinguish the separate idea of God. Before to-day I do not think I have ever realized that God was distinct from Jesus. It enlarges the matter almost beyond comprehension. People doubt the existence of Jesus – at least, they doubt incidents of his life, such as, say, the Ascension into Heaven after his death. But I do not understand that they deny God. I think everyone admits that in some form or other. – The thought makes the world sweeter – even if God be no more than the mystery of Life.

WALLACE STEVENS
Letters of Wallace Stevens

We All Pick and Choose

In 19 centuries not one of all his followers has quite in all points agreed with Christ.

RICHARD JEFFERIES
Notebooks

The Enemy of Progress

You find as you look round the world that every single bit of progress in human feeling, every improvement in the criminal law, every step towards the diminution of war, every step towards better treatment of the coloured races, or every miti-gation of slavery, every moral progress that has been in the world, has been consistently opposed by the organized Churches of the world. I say quite deliberately that the Christian religion, as organized in its Churches, has been and still is the principal enemy of moral progress in the world.

BERTRAND RUSSELL
Why I Am Not A Christian

The Errors of Crosstianity

To
Unidentified Correspondent

4 Whitehall Court sw1
12th June 1931.

Your sermon interests me only as an example of the lengths to which 'Crosstian' apologists will go in their quite hopeless attempts to whitewash the Roman gibbet. What do you expect me to say to such a mad remark as that 'In the Cross we see God's love in action'? If by God you mean the fabulous Ogre who sought to be propitiated by human sacrifices by Abraham and Jephtha what has love to do with the affair? If you mean the God whom Jesus addressed when He cried 'Why has thou forsaken me?' you suggest very strongly that the only possible answer was 'Alas my poor friend, because I have no other instrument than yourself and those who think like you; and it seems that my enemies are too many for you.' But you must not muddle up the two and write nonsense to me. It is that sort of nonsense that drives people out of the churches.

Also I wish you would read the Gospels in a sane manner and not indulge in such inventions as that Jesus might have saved himself by recanting or might have rescued himself by force. He had no loophole for escape by way of recantation; as to force, if you really believe as a silly passage in St John's Gospel suggests, that he had only to lift his finger to make the whole Roman army of occupation, with Pilate, Caiaphas and the Sanhedrin fall flat on the ground, you are not only giving up the whole business as a fairy tale, but provoking the question why, in that case, did he not do it and thereby give the world an overwhelming demonstration of his powers instead of exposing himself to the mockery of the Jews 'He saved others: Himself He cannot save. Let Him deliver him if He delight in him.'

It is quite clear from the Gospel narrative that Jesus connived at his own death in the belief that he would rise again and come to glory to establish his reign on earth. Subsequent history has not confirmed his belief. If Christianity means ignoring history and perpetuating his delusion it has no future. If it means a serious attempt to popularize what is still valuable in Christ's ideas then he may really yet come to his own after centuries of failure. It may be that Crosstianity has made him such a bore, and so associated his name with manifest falsehood and superstition that his ideas can be preserved only by suppressing his connection with them. But, anyhow, don't insult him by saying that the whole value of his life would have been destroyed if he had not been hideously tortured and slaughtered.

GEORGE BERNARD SHAW
Collected Letters, Vol. IV

TEACHINGS

Vitality the Overriding Virtue

In the Lutheran Sunday school I attended as a child, a large reproduction of a popular painting in a milky Germanic Victorian style showed a robed Jesus praying in Gethsemane, his hands folded on a conveniently tablelike rock, his lightly bearded face turned upward with a melancholy radiance as he asked, presumably, for this cup to pass from him, and listened to the heavenly refusal. I was a mediocre Sunday-school student, who generally failed to win the little perfect-attendance pin in May. But I was impressed by the saying that to lust after a woman in your heart is as bad as actual adultery and deserving of self-mutilation, because it posited a world, co-existent with that of trees and automobiles and living people around me, in which a motion of the mind, of the soul, was an actual deed, as important as a physical act. And I took in the concept that God watches the sparrow's fall – that our world is everywhere, at all times, in every detail, watched by God, like a fourth dimension. Some of the parables – the one in which the prodigal son received favorable treatment, or those in which foolish virgins or ill-paid vineyard workers are left to wail in outer darkness – puzzled and repelled me, in their sketches of the dreadful freedom that reigns behind God's dispensations, but the parable of the talents bore a clear lesson: Live your life. Live it as if there is a blessing on it. Dare to take chances, lest you leave your talent buried in the ground. I could picture so clearly the hole that the timorous servant would dig in the dirt, and even imagine how cozily cool and damp it would feel to his hand as he placed his talent in it.

Like millions of other little citizens of Christendom I was infected with the dangerous idea that there is a double standard, this world's and another's, and that the other is higher, and all true life flows from it. Vitality perhaps, is the overriding virtue in the Bible; the New Testament, for all its legalisms, obscurities, repetitions, and dark patches, renews the vitality of the Old. From certain verbal prominences, burnished by ages of quotation like kissed toes on bronze statues of saints, and from certain refracting facets of the tumbled testamental matter a light shuddered forth which corresponded, in my consciousness as a child, to the vibrant, uncourted moments of sheer happiness that I occasionally experienced. I still have them, these visitations of joy and gratitude, and still associate them with the Good News. 'Know too,' Matthew's Gospel ends, 'that I am with you every day to the end of time.'

JOHN UPDIKE
'St Matthew's Gospel', from *Odd Jobs*

Horrifying

'Lay not up for yourselves treasures upon earth, where moth and rust doth corrupt, and where thieves break through and steal; but lay up for yourselves treasures in heaven, where neither moth nor rust doth corrupt and where thieves do not break through nor steal; for where your treasure is there will your heart be also.' (Matthew 6: 19-21)

... impossible to imagine a statement more explicit, or more horrifying to the average man of this world.

UPTON SINCLAIR
A Personal Jesus

A Religion of Kindliness

It is curious how bold some very ordinary statements seem when they are put into print in a popular newspaper. I do not believe, and never have at any time believed, in the divinity of Christ, the Virgin Birth, the Immaculate Conception, heaven, hell, the immortality of the soul, the divine inspiration of the Bible. These denials of belief are taken for granted in the conversation of the vast majority of my friends and acquaintance. And, far from seeming bold, they are so commonplace to us that we very rarely trouble to repeat them, much less argue about them ...

Of all the Oriental creeds of which I have knowledge, the Christian creed is to me the least satisfactory, save only that of Mohammedanism. (It should be remembered that the Christian creed is Oriental. Every Occidental creed in Europe has died out.) On the other hand, the moral teaching of Christ makes a most powerful appeal to me, and I should not care to assert that in the field of morals Christ was not the greatest man that ever lived ...

It seems to me that Christ better than anybody understood the secret of happiness, which is the avowed end of all religious beliefs. Christ taught an all-embracing sympathy. He taught humility, meekness. he taught us to judge not that we be not judged. He taught forgiveness. he taught the return of good for evil. In a word, his religion was, in practice, the religion of kindliness.

I do not hold that kindliness comprises the whole of 'works', and that nothing else matters. Far from it. But I do hold that without kindliness, mercy, humility, forgiveness, and such acts as the suffering of fools gladly, no amount of 'works' can be effective, or have any real value in a religious sense . . .

ARNOLD BENNETT

My Religion

⟞⟝

One of the Most Important Sayings

'Judge not that ye be not judged' – one of the most important and significant sayings in the whole corpus of Jesus' teachings.

ALDOUS HUXLEY

Letters

⟞⟝

Jesus the Poet

I see a far more intimate and immediate connection between the true life of Christ and the true life of the artist; and I take a keen pleasure in the reflection that long before sorrow had made my days her own and bound me to her wheel I had written in The Soul of Man that he who would lead a Christlike life must be entirely and absolutely himself, and had taken as my types not merely the shepherd on the hillside and the prisoner in his cell, but also the painter to whom the world is a pageant and the poet for whom the world is a song. I remember saying once to Andre Gide, as we sat together in some Paris cafe, that while metaphysics had but little real interest for me, and morality absolutely none, there was nothing that either Plato or Christ had said that could not be transferred immediately into the sphere of Art and there find its complete fulfilment.

Nor is it merely that we can discern in Christ that close union of personality with perfection which forms the real distinction between the classical and romantic movement in life, but the very basis of his nature was the same as that of the nature of the artist – an intense and flamelike imagination. He realised in the entire sphere of human relations that imaginative sympathy which in the sphere of Art is that sole secret of creation. He understood the leprosy of the leper, the darkness of the blind, the fierce misery of whose who live for pleasure, the strange poverty in the rich. Someone wrote to me in trouble, 'When you are not on your pedestal you are not interesting'. How remote was that writer from what Matthew Arnold calls 'the Secret of Jesus'. Either would have taught him that whatever happens to another happens to oneself, and if you want an inscription to read at dawn and at night-time, and for pleasure or for pain, write up on the walls of your house in letters for the sun to gild and the moon to silver, 'Whatever happens to oneself happens to another'.

Christ's place indeed is with the poets. His whole conception of humanity sprang right out of the imagination and can only be realised by it. What God was to the pantheist, a man was to him. He was the first to conceive the divided races as a unity. Before his time there had been gods and men, and, feeling through the mysticism of sympathy that in himself each had been made incarnate, he calls himself the Son of the one or the Son of the other, according to his mood. More than anyone else in history he wakes in us that temper of wonder to which romance always appeals. There is still something to me almost incredible in the idea of a Galilean peasant imagining that he could bear on his shoulders the burden of the entire world: all that had already been done and suffered, and all that was yet to be done and suffered: the sins of Nero, of Caesar Borgia, of Alexander VI, and of him who was Emperor of Rome and Priest of the Sun: the sufferings of those whose names are legion and whose dwelling is among the tombs: oppressed nationalities, factory children, thieves, people in prison, out-casts, those who are dumb under oppression and whose silence is heard only of God; and not merely imagining this but actually achieving it, so that at the present moment all who come in contact with his personality, even though they may neither bow to his altar nor kneel before his priest, in some way find that the ugliness of their sin is taken away and the beauty of their sorrow revealed to them.

I had said of Christ that he ranks with the poets. That is true. Shelley and Sophocles are of his company. But his entire life also is the most wonderful of poems. For 'pity and terror' there is nothing in the entire cycle of Greek tragedy to touch it. The absolute purity of the protagonist raises the entire scheme to a height of romantic art from which the sufferings of Thebes and Pelops' line are by their very horror excluded, and shows how wrong Aristotle was when he said in his treatise on the drama that it would be impossible to bear the spectacle of one blame-less in pain. Nor in Æschylus nor Dante, those stern masters of tenderness, in Shakespeare, the most purely human of all the great artists, in the whole of Celtic myth and legend, where the loveliness of the world is shown through a mist of tears, and the life of man no more than the life of a flower, is there anything that, for sheer simplicity of pathos wedded and made one with sublimity of tragic effect, can be said to equal or even approach the last act of Christ's passion. The little supper with his companions, one of whom has already sold him for a price; the anguish in the quiet moonlit garden; the false friend who still believed in him, and on whom as on a rock he had hoped to build a house of refuge for Man, denying him as the bird cried to the dawn; his own utter loneliness, his submission, his acceptance of everything; and along with it all such scenes as the high priest of orthodoxy rending his raiment in wrath, and the magistrate of civil justice calling for water in the vain hope of cleansing himself of that stain of innocent blood that makes him the scarlet figure of history; the coronation ceremony of sorrow, one of the most wonderful things in the whole of recorded time; the crucifixion of the Innocent One before the eyes of his mother and of the disciple whom he loved; the soldiers gambling and throwing dice for his clothes; the terrible death by which he gave the world its most eternal symbol; and his final burial in the tomb of the rich man, his body swathed in Egyptian linen with costly spices and perfumes as though he had been a king's son. When one contemplates all this from the point of view of art alone one cannot but be grateful that the supreme office of the Church should be playing of the tragedy without the shedding of blood: the mystical presentation, by means of dialogue and costume and gesture even, of the Passion of her Lord; and it is always a source of pleasure and awe to me to remember that the ultimate survival of the Greek chorus, lost elsewhere to art, is to be found in the servitor answering the priest at Mass.

. . .

If ever I write again, in the sense of producing artistic work, there are just two subjects on which and through which I desire to express myself: one is 'Christ as the precursor of the romantic movement in life': the other is 'The artistic life considered in its relation to conduct'. The first is, of course, intensely fascinating, for I see in Christ not merely the essentials of the supreme romantic type, but all the accidents, the wilfulnesses even, of the romantic temperament also. He was the first person who ever said to people that they should live 'flowerlike lives'. He fixed the phrase. He took children as the type of what people should try to become. He held them up as examples to their elders, which I myself have always thought the chief use of children, if what is perfect should have a use. Dante describes the soul of man as coming from the hand of God 'weeping and laughing like a little child', and Christ also saw that the soul of each one should be *a guisa di fanciulla che piangendo e ridendo pargoleggia.* He felt that life was changeful, fluid, active, and that to allow it to be stereotyped into any form was death. He saw that people should not be too serious over material, common interests; that to be unpractical was to be a great thing: that one should not bother too much over affairs. The birds didn't, why should man? He is charming when he says, 'Take no thought for the morrow; is not the soul more than meat? is not the body more than raiment?' A Greek might have used the latter phrase. It is full of Greek feeling. But only Christ could have said both, and so summed up life perfectly for us.

His morality is all sympathy, just what morality should be. If the only thing that he ever said had been, 'Her sins are forgiven her because she loved much,' it would have been worth while dying to have said it. His justice is all poetical justice, exactly what justice should be. The beggar goes to heaven because he has been unhappy. I cannot conceive a better reason for his being sent there. The people who work for an hour in the vineyard in the cool of the evening receive just as much reward as those who have toiled there all day long in the hot sun. Why shouldn't they? Probably no one deserved anything. Or perhaps they were a different kind of people. Christ had no patience with the dull lifeless mechanical systems that treat people as if they were things, and so treat everybody alike: for him there were no laws: there were exceptions merely, as if anybody, or anything, for that matter, was like aught else in the world!

That which is the very keynote of romantic art was to him the proper basis of natural life. He saw no other basis. And when they brought him one taken in the very act of sin and showed him her sentence written in the law, and asked him what was to be done, he wrote with his finger on the ground as though he did not hear them, and finally, when they pressed him again, looked up and said, 'Let him of you who has never sinned be the first to throw the stone at her'. It was worth while living to have said that.

Like all poetical natures he loved ignorant people. He knew that in the soul of one who is ignorant there is always room for a great idea. But he could not stand stupid people, especially those who are made stupid by education: people who are full of opinions not one of which they even understand, a peculiarly modern type, summed up by Christ when he describes it as the type of one who has the key of knowledge, cannot use it himself, and does not allow other people to use it, though it may be made to open the gate of God's Kingdom. His chief war was against the Philistines. That is the war every child of light has to wage. Philistinism was the note of the age and community in which he lived. In their heavy inaccessibility to ideas, their dull respectability, their tedious orthodoxy, their worship of vulgar success, their entire preoccupation with the gross materialistic side of life, and their ridiculous estimate of themselves and their importance, the Jews of Jerusalem in Christ's day were the exact counterpart of the British Philistinism of our own. Christ mocked at the 'whited sepulchre' of respectability, and fixed that phrase for ever. He treated worldly success as a thing absolutely to be despised. He saw nothing in it at all. He looked on wealth as an encumbrance to a man. he would not hear of life being sacrificed to any system of thought or morals. He pointed out that forms and ceremonies were made for man, not man for forms ceremonies. He took sabbatarianism as a type of the things that should be set at nought. The cold philanthropies, the ostentatious public charities, the tedious formalisms so dear to the middle-class mind, he exposed with utter and relentless scorn. To us, what is termed orthodoxy is merely a facile unintelligent acquiescence; but to them, and in their hands, it was a terrible and paralysing tyranny. Christ swept it aside. He showed that the spirit alone was of value. He took a keen pleasure in pointing out to them that though they were always reading the law and the prophets, they had not really the smallest idea of what either of them meant. In opposition to their tithing of each separate day into the fixed routine of prescribed duties, as they tithe mint and rue, he preached the enormous importance of living completely for the moment.

Those whom he saved from their sins are saved simply for beautiful moments in their lives. Magdalen, when she sees Christ, breaks the rich vase of alabaster that one of her seven lovers had given her, and spills the odorous spices over his tired dusty feet, and for that one moment's sake sits forever with Ruth and Beatrice in the tresses of the snow-white rose of Paradise. All that Christ says to us by the way of a little warning is that every moment should be beautiful, that the soul should always be ready for the coming of the bridegroom, always waiting for the voice of the lover, Philistinism being simply that side of man's nature that is not illumined by the imagination. He sees all the lovely influences of life as modes of light: the imagination itself is the world of light. The world is made by it, and yet the world cannot understand it: that is because imagination is simply a manifestation of love, and it is love and the capacity for it that distinguishes one human being from another.

But it is when he deals with a sinner that Christ is most romantic, in the sense of most real. The world has always loved the saint as being the nearest possible approach to the perfection of God. Christ through some divine instinct in him, seems to have always loved the sinner as being the nearest possible approach to the perfection of man. His primary desire was not to reform people, any more than his primary desire was to relieve suffering. To turn an interesting thief into a tedious honest man was not his aim. He would have thought little of the Prisoners Aid Society and other modern movements of the kind. The conversion of a publican into a Pharisee would not have seemed to him a great achievement. But in a manner not yet understood of the world he regarded sin and suffering as being in themselves beautiful holy things and modes of perfection.

It seems a very dangerous idea. It is – all great ideas are dangerous. That it was Christ's creed admits of no doubt. That is the true creed I don't doubt myself.

Of course the sinner must repent. But why? Simply because otherwise he would be unable to realise what he had done. The moment of repentance is the moment of initiation. More than that: it is the means by which one alters one's past. The Greeks thought that impossible. They often say in their gnomic aphorisms,

'Even the Gods cannot alter the past'. Christ showed that the commonest sinner could do it, that it was the one thing he could do. Christ, had he been asked, would have said – I feel quite certain about it – that the moment the prodigal son fell on his knees and wept, he made his having wasted his substance with harlots, his swine-herding and hungering for the husks they ate, beautiful and holy moments in his life. It is difficult for most people to grasp the idea. I daresay one has to go to prison to understand it. If so, it may be worth while going to prison.

There is something so unique about Christ. Of course just as there are false dawns before the dawn itself, and winter days so full of sudden sunlight that they will cheat the wise crocus into squandering its gold before its time, and make some foolish bird call its mate to build on barren boughs, so there were Christians before Christ. For that we should be grateful. The unfortunate thing is that there have been none since. I make one exception, St Francis of Assisi. But then God had given him at his birth the soul of a poet, as he himself when quite young had in mystical marriage taken poverty as his bride; and with the soul of a poet and the body of a beggar he found the way to him. We do not require the Liber Conformitatum to teach us that the life of St Francis was the true *Imitatio Christi,* a poem compared to which the book of that name is merely prose.

Indeed, that is the charm about Christ, when all is said: he is just like a work of art. He does not really teach one anything, but by being brought into his presence one becomes something. And everybody is predestined to his prescience. Once at least in his life each man walks with Christ to Emmaus.

OSCAR WILDE
De Profundis

Exceedingly Affecting

He repeated to Mr Langton, with great energy, in the Greek, our Saviour's gracious expression concerning the forgiveness of Mary Magdalen: 'Thy faith have saved thee: go in peace.' He said, 'the manner of this dismissal is exceedingly affecting.'

DR JOHNSON
quoted in Boswell's *Life of Samuel Johnson*

Jesus and Marx

'My, oh my. Jesus was really pretty radical. One place where Marx and Jesus meet is that each believed that money leaches out all other values.'

NORMAN MAILER
Waterstones Magazine

Better Than Marx

Only a revolution that overthrows the meanness in the minds of men is real, all the rest are masquerades, the only real thing about them is their bullets. It may indeed be impossible for everyone to lead a good life on this earth. It may not be in the cards, but no one has a right to stop us from re-shuffling those cards from time to time. Everybody should have enough, and enough for each person is not necessarily the same amount. Yet anybody who has more than another needs has too much. This is especially true when insults are being handed out. I will take equality with me but freedom is the place to where I am going. This idea reached its height in the life of Jesus of Nazareth.

And up until the time that it is permanently achieved, its most permanent form is in His teachings. There is as much socialism in the Sermon on the Mount as there is in the Communist Manifesto and better prose. For He told the laughed-at, the insulted and those they jeer, that they were kings and that their kingdoms were waiting for them inside themselves. He was a harp on which the finest poetry of which the human heart is capable played out its necessity and its need. If anyone doubts this, I hope this language will give me a reference. For truth is more important than infallibility and truer. And don't ever forget that a slave is always a free man in chains.

PAUL POTTS
To Keep a Promise

Resist Not Evil

There is a short prayer which is often employed by members of Alcoholics Anonymous. It goes thus: 'God grant us the serenity to accept the things we cannot change, courage to change the things we can, and wisdom to know the difference.'

To get to the crux of the problem, which had become almost obsessive, here is what we asked each other: 'Can one really aid another individual, and if so, how?'

The question was answered, of course, long ago by Jesus in a simple, direct way, one which today we are prone to call a Zen-like way. Jesus made a number of explicit statements, injunctions really. All to the effect that one was to take no thought but to respond immediately to any appeal for aid. And to respond in large measure. To give your cloak as well as your coat, to walk two miles and not one. And as we know well, with these injunctions went another, more important one – to return good for evil. 'Resist not evil!'

Throughout the parables of Jesus there is implicit another most wholesome idea, that we are not to seek trouble, not to go about trying to patch things up, not to endeavour to convert others to our way of thinking, but to demonstrate the truth which is in us by acting instinctively and spontaneously when confronted with an issue. To do our part and trust in the Lord, in other words.

By responding with a full spirit to any demand which is made upon us we aid our fellow man to help himself. For Jesus there was no problem involved. It was simple. By giving the full measure of oneself – more, in other words, than was demanded – you restored to the one in need his human dignity. You gave from the cup that was overflowing. The need of the other instantly vanished. Because it was met by the inexhaustible reservoir of spirit. And spirit answers to spirit.

HENRY MILLER
Stand Still Like the Hummingbird

A Prophet Called Christ

Although I don't believe in Christ the son of God, I certainly believe there was a prophet called Christ, and the best thing he ever said was that a rich man cannot have any happiness at all because of the constant worry. The thing about being poor is that you don't need to worry; things can only get better.

SIMON RAVEN
quoted in the *Oldie* magazine

Jesus Opposes Courts of Justice

In Luke (vi. 39–49) these very words are said, immediately after those which teach us not to resist evil, but to return good for evil. Immediately after the words, 'Be ye merciful, even as your father is merciful,' it is said, 'And judge not, and ye shall not be judged: and condemn not, and ye shall not be condemned.' Does not this mean, said I to myself, that not only should we not condemn our neighbour verbally, but that tribunals for the judgment of our neighbourhoods are not to be established? It was only necessary for me to put the question, and both my heart and common sense at once answered it in the affirmative.

I know well how startling is such an interpretation of these words at first. Certainly it startled me. To show how far I was from a right understanding, I will confess to a shameful piece of foolishness. Even after I had become a believer, and had read the Gospel as a divine book, when I met my friends among lawyers and judges, by way of a playful joke I would say to them, 'So you still keep on judging, and yet it is said, "Judge not, that ye be not judged."' I felt so certain that these words could have been uttered only against slander and the like that I did not understand the horrible sacrilege of which I myself was guilty. I had come to this, that persuaded these clear words meant something other than they do, I had in jest used them in their true significance.

I will relate in detail how all my doubts about the meaning of these words were removed; how I came to perceive that they could mean nothing but that Christ forbade all earthly tribunals of justice, and that when he made use of them, that, and that only, must have been his meaning.

The first thing which astounded me, when I had understood the commandment of non-resistance to evil in its simple sense, was that earthly courts of justice, not only are not in accordance with it, but are directly contrary to it, contrary also to the spirit of the whole teaching, and that consequently if Christ thought of these tribunals he must have condemned them.

Christ says, Resist not evil: the objects of the courts is to resist evil. Christ says, Return good for evil: the courts render evil for evil. Christ says, Do not classify men as good or bad; the courts are occupied only in making this distinction. Christ says, forgive all men; forgive not once, not seven times, but without end; love your enemies, do good to those that hate you: the courts do not forgive, but punish; they render not good but evil to those whom they call the enemies of society.

LEO TOLSTOY
What I Believe

The Secret of Christ

'Know Thyself' was written over the portal of the antique world. Over the portal of the new world, 'Be thyself' shall be written. And the message of Christ to man was simply 'Be thyself.' That is the secret of Christ.

OSCAR WILDE
The Soul of Man Under Socialism

What Does it Matter Whether He Was Tall or Short

It is the words of Jesus which compel our attention, and it is in his words that we initially meet him. The New Testament commentaries abound in references to the Old Testament, to the Jewish Apocrypha, to the Dead Sea Scrolls, to Philo, designed to show us how much Jesus had in common with his antecedents and his contemporaries. It would be very surprising if he did not have *something* in common with the tradition and setting from which he sprang. But it would be a denial of history, a denial of the experience of countless men and women throughout the centuries, if one thought that *all* the sayings of Jesus were little more than a first century semitic pot-pourri. They are blindingly and terrifyingly different from anything that anyone has ever said before or since: in their absolutism, and, at first sight, in their mercilessness. G.K. Chesterton, in *The Everlasting Man,* remarks that the Christ of the Gospels 'might seem actually more strange and terrible than the Christ of the Church'. This is surely a just description of One who could tell human beings that their most blessed condition was one of abject poverty; of one who recommended, in a doubtless metaphorical sense, that if our hand offends us we should cut it off; of one who terrified the demons in the Gerasene lunatics and sent the herd of pigs screaming over the cliff; of one who promised his disciples that they would be 'hated by all men because you bear my name'; of one who said that he came to bring a sword, not peace:

> I have come to set a man at variance with his father, and the daughter with her mother, and the daughter-in-law with her mother-in-law; a man's enemies will be the people of his own house. He is not worthy of me, that loves father or mother more; he is not worthy of me, that loves son or daughter more; he is not worthy of me that does not take up his cross and follow me.

He who secures his own life will lose it; it is the man who loses his life for my sake that will secure it.

(Matthew 10:35–40)

We can say a lot about the man who said those words. But what we can't say is that we do not know anything about him. What does it matter whether he was tall or short or fat or thin or married or unmarried or a carpenter or a rabbi? The words shout at you. If an individual saying or logion finds its parallel in some other place, the effect of the whole collection of sayings is unmistakable. His words stand all our ordinary worldly standards of common sense on their heads. We can characterise almost all his utterances as being of this essentially paradoxical kind. If we wish to gain life, we must lose it. If we wish to lay up treasure in heaven, we must be poor. However the various redactors or evangelists have arranged the sayings, and whatever the difficulty of understanding how individual sayings apply, the manifesto for the Kingdom is unmistakably disturbing. The words which are attributed to him by all the Gospel-writers proclaim him as a figure wholly at variance with the wisdom of the world. 'My kingdom does not belong to this world', Saint John has him saying to Pilate, when the whole conflict has reached its climax.

A.N. WILSON

How Can We Know?

The Greatest Thing

Christ said that the greatest thing a man could do was to give up his own life to save that of a friend. Now the greatest poem in the whole Christian civilization, greater than the idea in Faust, is for a person to be willing to lose his own soul, to go to hell for all eternity, to save the soul of someone he loved.

Even the most beautiful Christian in all history, even St Francis of Assisi, would call this heresy. But I'm certainly a heretic when I think of the woman I love.

PAUL POTTS
Dante Called You Beatrice

Magnificent Menace

The statement that the meek shall inherit the earth is very far from being a meek statement. I mean it is not meek in the ordinary sense of mild and moderate and inoffensive. To justify it, it would be necessary to go very deep into history and anticipate things undreamed of then and by many unrealised even now; such as the way in which the mystical monks reclaimed the lands which the practical kings had lost. If it was a truth at all, it was because it was a prophecy. But certainly it was not a truth in the sense of a truism. The blessing upon the meek would seem to be a very violent statement; in the sense of doing violence to reason and probability. And with this we come to another important stage in the speculation. As a prophecy it really was fulfilled; but it was only fulfilled long afterwards. The monasteries were the most practical and prosperous estates and experiments in reconstruction after the barbaric deluge; the meek really did inherit the earth. But nobody could have known anything of the sort at the time – unless indeed there was one who knew. Something of the same thing may be said about the incident of Martha and Mary; which has been interpreted in retrospect and from the inside by the mystics of the Christian contemplative life. But it was not all an obvious view of it; and most moralists, ancient and modern, could be trusted to make a rush for the obvious. What torrents of effortless eloquence would have flowed from them to swell any slight superiority on the part of Martha; what splendid sermons about the Joy of

Service and the Gospel of Work and the World Left Better Than We Found It, and generally all the ten thousand platitudes than can be uttered in favour of taking trouble – by people who need take no trouble to utter them. If in Mary the mystic and child of love Christ was guarding the seed of something more subtle, who was likely to understand it at the time? Nobody else could have seen Clare and Catherine and Teresa shining above the little roof at Bethany. It is so in another way with that magnificent menace about bringing into the world a sword to sunder and divide. Nobody could have guessed then either how it could be fulfilled or how it could be justified. Indeed some freethinkers are still so simple as to fall into the trap and be shocked at a phrase so deliberately defiant. They actually complain of the paradox for not being a platitude.

G.K. CHESTERTON
The Essential G.K. Chesterton

Eternal Torment

Why will no Christian face the savage and vindictive fit of rage into which the New Testament Jesus so often fell, promising eternal torment to all who rejected him?

PHILIP TOYNBEE
End of a Journey

Jesus the Socialist

When Jesus talks about the poor he simply means personalities, just as when he talks about the rich he simply means people who have not developed their personalities. Jesus moved in a community that allowed the accumulation of private property just as ours does, and the gospel that he preached was not that in such a community it is an advantage for a man to live on scanty, unwholesome food, to wear ragged, unwholesome clothes, to sleep in horrid, unwholesome dwellings, and a disadvantage for a man to live under healthy, pleasant and decent conditions. Such a view would have been wrong there and then, and would of course be still more wrong now and in England; for as a man moves northwards the material necessities of life become of more vital importance, and our society is infinitely more complex, and displays far greater extremes of luxury and pauperism than any society of the antique world. What Jesus meant, was this. He said to man, 'You have a wonderful personality. Develop it. Be yourself. Don't imagine that your perfection lies in accumulating or possessing external things. Your perfection is inside of you. If only you could realise that, you would not want to be rich. Ordinary riches can be stolen from a man. Real riches cannot. In the treasury-house of your soul, there are infinitely precious things, that may not be taken from you. And so try to shape your life that external things will not harm you. And try also to get rid of personal property. It involves sordid preoccupation, endless industry, continual wrong. Personal property hinders Individualism at every step.' It is to be noted that Jesus never says that impoverished people are necessarily good, or wealthy people necessarily bad. That would not have been true. Wealthy people are, as a class, better than impoverished people, more moral, more intellectual, more well-behaved. *There is only one class in the community that thinks more about money than the rich, and that is the poor.* The poor can think of nothing else. That is the misery of being poor. What Jesus does say is that man reaches his perfection, not through what he has, not even through what he does, but entirely through what he is. And so the wealthy young man who comes to Jesus is represented as a thoroughly good citizen, who has broken none of the laws of his state, none of the commandments of his religion. He is quite respectable, in the ordinary sense of that extraordinary word. Jesus says to him, 'You should give up private property. It hinders you from realising your perfection. It is a drag within you, and not outside of you, that you will find what you really are and what you really want.' To his own friends he says the same thing. He tells them to be themselves, and not to be always worrying about other things. What do other things matter? Man is complete in himself. When they go into the world, the world will disagree with them. That is inevitable. The world hates individualism. But this is not to trouble them. They are to be calm and self-centred. If a man takes their cloak, they are to give him their coat, just to show that material things are of no importance. If people abuse them, they are not to answer back. What does it signify? The things people say of a man do not alter a man. He is what he is. Public opinion is of no value whatsoever. Even if people employ actual violence, they are not to be violent in turn. That would be to fall to the same low level. After all, even in prison, a man can be quite free. His soul can be free. His personality can be untroubled. he can be at peace. And, above all things, they are not to interfere with other people or judge them in any way. Personality is a very mysterious thing. A man cannot always be estimated by what he does. He may keep the law, and yet be worthless. He may break the law, and yet be fine. He may be bad, without ever doing anything bad. He may commit a sin against society, and yet realise through that sin his true perfection.

There was a woman who was taken in adultery. We are not told the history of her love, but that love must have been very great; for Jesus said that her sins were forgiven her, not because she repented, but because her love was so intense and wonder-ful. Later on, a short time before his death, as he sat at a feast, the woman came in and poured costly perfumes on his hair. His friends tried to interfere with her, and said that it was an extravagance, and that the money that the perfume cost should have been expended on charitable relief of people in want, or something of that kind. Jesus did not accept that view. He pointed out that the material needs of Man were great and very permanent, but that the spiritual needs of Man were greater still, and that in one divine moment, and by selecting its own mode of expression, a personality might make itself perfect. The world worships the woman, even now, as a saint.

Yes, there are suggestive things in Individualism. Socialism annihilates family life for instance. With the abolition of private property, marriage in its present form must disappear. This is part of the programme. Individualism accepts this and makes it fine. It converts the abolition of legal restraint into a form of freedom that will help the full development of personality, and make the love of man and woman more wonderful, more beautiful, and more ennobling. Jesus knew this. He rejected the claims of family life, although they existed in his day and community in a very marked form. 'Who is my mother? Who are my brothers?' he said, when he was told that they wished to speak to him. When one of his followers asked to leave to go and bury his father, 'Let the dead bury the dead,' was his terrible answer. He would allow no claim whatsoever to be made on personality.

OSCAR WILDE
The Soul of Man Under Socialism

Profound Wisdom

The Being who has influenced in the most memorable manner the opinions and the fortunes of the human species is Jesus Christ. At this day his name is connected with the devotional feelings of two hundred millions of the race of man. The institutions of the most civilized portion of the globe derive their authority from the sanction of his doctrines, his invincible gentleness, and benignity, the devoted love borne to him by his adherents suggested a persuasion to them that he was something divine. The supernatural events which the historians of this wonderful man subsequently asserted to have been connected with every gradation of his career established the opinion. His death is said to have been accompanied by an accumulation of tremendous prodigies. Utter darkness fell upon the earth, blotting the noonday sun, dead bodies arising from their graves walked through the public streets, and an earthquake shook the astonished city, rending the rocks of the surrounding mountains. The philosophers may attribute the application of these events *to* the death of a reformer or the events themselves to a visitation of that Universal Pan who may be a God or man. It is the profound wisdom and the comprehensive morality of his doctrines which essentially distinguished him from the crowd of martyrs and of patriots who have exulted to devote themselves for what they conceived would contribute to the benefit of their fellowmen.

PERCY BYSSHE SHELLEY
Shelley's Prose

Death is Ever on the Watch

In Luke (xiv. 28–31) we find, 'For which of you, desiring to build a tower, doth not first sit down and count the cost, whether he have wherewith to complete it? Lest haply, when he hath laid a foundation, and is not able to finish, all that behold begin to mock him, saying, This man began to build, and was not able to finish. Or what king, as he goeth to encounter another king in war, will not sit down first and take counsel whether he is able with ten thousand to meet him that cometh against him with twenty thousand?'

Is it not, then, a senseless thing to take pains with what, for all your labour, will never be finished? Death will always come before the house of your earthly happiness is completed. And if you know beforehand, that however you may struggle against the death, the victory will be to him and not to you, is it not better to cease to struggle with him, to set all your affections not on that which must be of a certainty perish, but to seek that which death cannot affect?

In Luke (xii. 22–27) we read, 'And he said unto his disciples, Therefore I say unto you, Be not anxious for your life, what ye shall eat; nor yet for your body, what ye shall put on. For the life is more than the food, and the body than the raiment. Consider the ravens, that they sow not, neither reap; which have no store-chamber nor barn; and God feedeth them: of how much more value are ye than the birds! And which of you by being anxious can add a cubit to his stature? If, then, ye are not able to do even that which is least, why are ye anxious concerning the rest? Consider the lilies, how they grow: they toil not, neither do they spin; yet I say unto you, Even Solomon in all his glory was not arrayed like one of these.'

Whatever care you may take of your body and for your food, not one of you can add an hour to his life. Is it not, then, foolish to trouble ourselves with things over which you have no power?

You know well that your life must end in death, yet none the less you busy yourselves with guaranteeing your life by the possession of property. Life cannot be guaranteed by property. Understand, that this is an idle deceit with which you deceive yourselves.

The true significance of life lies not, says Christ, in what we have or what we get, in that which is without us. It must lie in something else.

He says (Luke xii. 16–21) that the life of man consists not in the abundance of his possessions. 'The ground of a certain rich man brought forth plentifully: and he reasoned within himself, saying, What shall I do, because I have not where to bestow my fruits? And he said, This will I do: I will pull down my barns, and build greater; and there I will bestow all my corn and my goods. And I will say to my soul, Soul, thou hast much goods laid up for many years; take thine ease, eat, drink, be merry. But God said unto him, Thou foolish one, this night is thy soul required of thee; and those things which thou hast prepared, whose shall they be? So is he that layeth up treasure for himself, and is not rich toward God.'

Death awaits us all at any and every moment. (Luke xii. 35–40): 'Let your loins be girded about, and your lamps burning: and be ye yourselves like unto men looking for their lord, when he shall return from the marriage feast; that, when he cometh and knocketh, they may straightaway open unto him. And if he shall come in the second watch, and if in the third, and find them so, blessed are those servants. But know this, that if the master of the house had known in what hour the thief was coming, he would have watched, and not have left his house to be broken through. Be ye also ready: for in an hour that ye think not the Son of man cometh.'

The parable of the virgins waiting for the coming of the bridegroom, of the end of time, and of the last judgment, all these passages, according to the opinion of all the commentators, besides their reference to the end of the world, are to remind us also of the nearness and the inevitableness of death.

Death is ever on the watch for you. Your life must be rounded in death. Even while you are working to lay up treasure for yourself in the future, you know that for you in the future there is only death, for you and for all that you have laboured for. Life, then, for life's sake, can have significance. If there be a life into which reason enters, it must be other than this one; it must be one whose aim is other than the laying up of treasure for the future. To live reasonably, is to live so that death cannot destroy life.

Christ says, in Luke (x. 41), 'Martha, Martha, thou art troubled about many things: but one thing is needful.'

All the innumerable cares with which we trouble ourselves for the future are useless; they are a delusion with which we mock ourselves. One thing only is needful.

From the day of his birth, inevitable ruin awaits man, a senseless life and a senseless death if he find not the one thing needful for the true life. What that one thing is Christ has told us. It is not of his own invention, nor does he promise to bestow it on us of his own divine power. He shows us only that together with the personal life, which has been proved a fallacy, there should be that which is a truth and no fallacy.

LEO TOLSTOY
What I Believe

Jesus Not a Christian

Christendom was torn by disputes about the Trinity. There is no evidence that the apostles of Jesus entertained that doctrine. Nor does he give his claim to be the 'Christ' or his participation in the Godhead any such prominence as one feels would have been done had he considered it a matter of primary significance. Most astounding is the statement (Matt. xvi.20) 'Then charged he his disciples that they should tell no man that he was Jesus the Christ!' It is difficult to understand this suppression if we suppose he considered this fact was essential to salvation.

The observance of the Jewish Sabbath, again, transferred to the Mithraic Sun-day, is an important feature of many Christian cults; but Jesus deliberately broke the Sabbath, and said that it was made for man and not man for the Sabbath. He did not say a word about the worship of his mother Mary, in the guise of

Isis, the Queen of Heaven. Much that is most characteristically Christian in worship and usage, he ignored. Sceptical writers have had the temerity to deny that Jesus can be called a Christian at all . . .

As remarkable is the enormous prominence given by Jesus to the teaching of what he called the Kingdom of Heaven, and its comparative insignificance in the procedure and teaching of most of the Christian churches.

This doctrine of the Kingdom of Heaven, which was the main teaching of Jesus, and which plays so small a part in the Christian creeds, is certainly one of the most revolutionary doctrines that ever stirred and changed human thought. It is small wonder if the world of that time failed to grasp its full significance, and recoiled in dismay from even a half-apprehension of its tremendous challenges to the established habits and institutions of mankind. It is small wonder if the hesitating convert and disciple presently went back to the old familiar ideas of temple and altar, of fierce deity and propitiatory observance, of consecrated priest and magic blessing, and – these things being attended to – reverted then to the dear old habitual life of hates and profits and competition and pride. For the doctrine of the Kingdom of Heaven, as Jesus seems to have preached it, was no less than a bold and uncompromising demand for a complete change and cleansing of the life of our struggling race, an utter cleansing, without and within . . .

The Jews were persuaded that God, the one God of the whole world, was a righteous god, but they also thought of Him as a trading god who had made a bargain with their Father Abraham about them, a very good bargain indeed for them, to bring them at last to predominance in the earth. With dismay and anger they heard Jesus sweeping away their dear securities. God, he taught, was no bargainer; there were no chosen people and no favourites in the Kingdom of Heaven. God was the loving father of all life, as incapable of showing favour as the universal sun. And all men were brothers – sinners alike and beloved sons alike – of this divine father. In the parable of the Good Samaritan Jesus cast scorn upon that natural tendency we all obey, to glorify our own people and to minimize the righteousness of other creeds and other races. In the parable of the labourers he thrust aside the obstinate claim of the Jews to have a sort of first mortgage upon God. All whom God takes into the kingdom, he taught, God serves alike; there is no distinction in His treatment, because there is no measure to his bounty. From all, moreover, as the parable of the buried talent witnesses, and as the incident of the widow's mite enforces, he demands the utmost. There are no privileges, no rebates, and no excuses in the Kingdom of Heaven.

But it is not only the intense tribal patriotism of the Jews that Jesus outraged. They were a people of intense family loyalty, and he would have swept away all the narrow and restrictive family affections in the great flood of love of God. The whole Kingdom of Heaven was to be the family of his followers. [Matt. xii. 46–50]

And not only did Jesus strike at patriotism and the bonds of family loyalty in the name of God's universal fatherhood and brotherhood of all mankind, but it is clear that his teaching condemned all the gradations of the economic system, all private wealth and personal advantages. All men belonged to the kingdom; all their possessions belonged to the kingdom; the righteous life for all men, the only righteous life, was the service of God's Will with all that we had, with all that we were. Again and again he denounced private riches and the reservation of any private life. [Mark x. 17–25]

Moreover, in his tremendous prophecy of this kingdom which was to make all men one together in God, Jesus had small patience for the bargaining righteousness of formal religion.

Another large part of his recorded utterances is aimed against the meticulous observance of the rules of the pious career. [Mark vii. 1–9]

So, too, we may note a score of places in which he flouted that darling virtue of the formalist, the observance of the Sabbath.

H.G. WELLS
A Short History of the World

MIRACLES

Not a Supernatural Personage

To Sister Laurentia McLachlan

If you could convince me that Jesus was a supernatural personage, as in his last distracted days he thought himself to be, I
should instantly lose all interest in him.

GEORGE BERNARD SHAW
Letters, Vol. IV

Moral Ills

In one respect alone have the miracles recorded by the Evangelists a more real ground than the mass of miracles of which we
have the relation. Medical science has never gauged, – never,
perhaps, enough set itself to gauge, – the intimate connexion
between moral fault and disease. To what extent, or in how
many cases, what is called *illness* is due to moral springs having
been used amiss, – whether by being over-used or by not being
used sufficiently, – we hardly at all know, and we far too little
inquire. Certainly it is due to this very much more than we
commonly think; and the more it is due to this, the more do
moral therapeutics rise in possibility and importance. The

bringer of light and happiness, the calmer and pacifier, or invigorator and stimulator, is one of the chiefest of doctors. Such a doctor was Jesus; such an operator, by an efficacious and real, though little observed and little employed agency, upon what we, in the language of popular superstition, call the *unclean spirits*, but which are to be designated more literally and more correctly as the *uncleared, unpurified spirits*, which came raging and madding before him. This his own language shows, if we know how to read it. *'What does it matter whether I say, Thy sins are forgiven thee! or whether I say, Arise and walk!'* And again: *'Thou art made whole; sin no more, lest a worse thing befall thee.'* His reporters, we must remember, are men who saw thaumaturgy in all that Jesus did, and who saw in all sickness and disaster visitations from God, and they bend his language accordingly. But indications enough remain to show the line of the Master, his perception of the large part of moral cause in many kinds of disease, and his method of addressing to this part his cure.

MATTHEW ARNOLD
Literature and Dogma

Cured by Faith

Healings were compelled from him, by acts of faith. When Jesus saw in men who cried to be cured, faith that his word would cure them, he spoke the word. He could not deny it. He could not deny it, because he loved, and more, because faith was what he was asking from men. Therefore he suffered men to heal themselves by faith in him. Yet even so, as the story of the palsied man shows plainly, the words he preferred to speak were words of healing of the soul. 'Your sins are forgiven.' The word of bodily healing was only wrung from him by the protests of the Scribes. He knew how easily, how inevitably, these words of his would cause him to be regarded as a worker of miracles; and how fatally his work would be distorted and encumbered. He trod the dangerous path warily. He pacified over-wrought minds, he suffered himself to speak the word to those 'whose faith had made them whole'; and in more than one crisis when there was no choice for it but to prove the truth of his own spiritual authority he spoke the word of healing before a concourse of people. When a man's faith had done the work, there Jesus spoke the word.

These were not prodigies: neither to Jesus, nor to us, nor to the men of his day. The gospels tell of many prodigies; but they tell also that after these prodigies had been performed, the religious Jews still asked for a sign, and Jesus still declared that no sign should be given them. It is plain as day that prodigies were not performed, but invented by a credulous after-generation. And again we need not seek a general definition of prodigy; the sufficient definition arises clearly from the story of Jesus himself. A prodigy was some strange and extraordinary happening that should compel men to believe him and his message. Jesus performed no sign that could compel men to believe in him. We know that he could not. But that is not very important. What is important is that he *would* not.

JOHN MIDDLETON MURRY
The Life of Jesus

Something of Very Little Importance

I am sure that Jesus *could* have walked on water quite easily, whether he did so or not. And that he would have regarded this feat as something of very little importance.

PHILIP TOYNBEE
End of a Journey

Peculiar to His Time

The truth is that, when critics have spoken of the local limitations of the Galilean, it has always been the case of the local
limitations of the critics. He did undoubtedly believe in certain
things that one particular modern sect of materialists do not
believe. But they were not things particularly peculiar to his
time. It would nearer the truth to say that the denial of them
is quite peculiar to our time. Doubtless it would be nearer still
to the truth to say merely that a certain solemn social importance, in the minority disbelieving them, is peculiar to our time.
He believed, for instance, in evil spirits or in the psychic healing
of bodily ills; but not because he was a Galilean born under
Augustus. It is absurd to say that a man believed things because
he was a Galilean under Augustus when he might have believed
the same things if he had been an Egyptian under Tutankhamen
or an Indian under Gengis Khan. But with this general question
of the philosophy of diabolism or of divine miracles I deal
elsewhere. It is enough to say that the materialists have to
prove the impossibility of miracles against the testimony of all
mankind, not against the prejudices of provincials in North
Palestine under the first Roman Emperors. What they have to
prove, for the present argument, is the presence in the Gospels
of those particular prejudices of those particular provincials.
And, humanly speaking, it is astonishing how little they can
produce even to make a beginning of proving it.

So it is in this case of the sacrament of marriage. We may
not believe in sacraments, as we may not believe in spirits, but
it is quite clear that Christ believed in this sacrament in his own
way and not in any current or contemporary way. He certainly
did not get his argument against divorce from the Mosaic law
or the Roman law or the habits of the Palestinian people. It
would appear to his critics then exactly what it appears to his

critics now; an arbitrary and transcendental dogma coming from nowhere save in the sense that it came from him. I am not at all concerned here to defend that dogma; the point here is that it is just as easy to defend it now as it was to defend it then. It is an ideal altogether outside time; difficult at any period; impossible at no period. In other words, if anyone says it is what might be expected of a man walking about in that place at that period, we can quite fairly answer that it is much *more* like what might be the mysterious utterance of a being beyond man, if he walked alive among men.

G.K. CHESTERTON
The Essential G.K. Chesterton

Evidence for Miracles

It will be noted by the older among my readers, who are sure to be obsessed more or less by elderly wrangles as to whether the gospels are credible as matter-of-fact narratives, that I have hardly raised this question, and have accepted the credible and incredible with equal complacency. I have done this because credibility is a subjective condition, as the evolution of religious belief clearly shews. Belief is not dependent on evidence and reason. There is as much evidence that the miracles occurred as that the battle of Waterloo occurred, or that a large body of Russian troops passed through England in 1914 to take part in the war on the western front. The reasons for believing in the murder of Pompey are the same as the reasons for believing in the raising of Lazarus. Both have been believed and doubted by men of equal intelligence. Miracles, in the sense of phenomena we cannot explain, surround us on every hand: life itself is the miracle of miracles. Miracles in the sense of events that violate the normal course of our experience are vouched for every day: the flourishing Church of Christ Scientist is founded on a multitude of such miracles. Nobody believes all the miracles: everybody believes some of them. I cannot tell why men who will not believe that Jesus ever existed yet believe firmly that Shakespear was Bacon. I cannot tell why people who believed that angels appeared and fought on our side at the battle of Mons, and who believe that miracles occur quite frequently at Lourdes, nevertheless boggle at the miracle of the liquefaction of the blood of St Januarius, and reject it as a trick of priestcraft. I cannot tell why people who will not believe Matthew's story of three kings bringing costly gifts to the cradle of Jesus, believe Luke's story of the shepherds and the stable. I cannot tell why people, brought up to believe the Bible in the old literal way as an infallible record and revelation, and rejecting that view later on, begin by rejecting the Old Testament, and give up belief in a brimstone hell before they give up (if they ever do) the belief in a heaven of harps, crowns, and thrones. I cannot tell why people who will not believe in baptism on any terms believe in vaccination with the cruel fanaticism of inquisitors. I am convinced that if a dozen sceptics were to draw up in parallel columns a list of the events narrated in the gospels which they consider credible and incredible respectively, their lists would be different in several particulars. Belief is literally a matter of taste.

GEORGE BERNARD SHAW
Preface to *Androcles and the Lion*

Jesus in Wonderland

Now, it may look at first sight a strange thing to say, but it is a truth which we will make abundantly clear as we go on, that one of the very best helps to prepare the way for valuing the Bible and believing in Jesus Christ, is to convince oneself of the liability to mistake in the Bible-writers. Our popular theology supposes that the Old Testament writers were miraculously inspired, and could make no mistakes; and that there there miraculous inspiration stopped, and all writers on religion have been liable to make mistakes ever since. It is as if a hand had been put out of the sky presenting us with the Bible, and the rules of criticism which apply to other books did not apply to the Bible. Now, the fatal thing for this supposition is, that its owners stab it to the heart the moment they use any palliation or explaining away, however small, of the literal words of the Bible; and *some* they always use. For instance it is said in the eighteenth Psalm, that a consuming fire went out of the mouth of God, so that coals were kindled at it. The veriest literalist will cry out: Everyone knows that this is not to be taken literally! The truth is, even *he* knows that *this* is not to be taken literally; but others know that a great deal more is not to be taken literally. He knows very little; but, as far as his little knowledge goes, he gives up his theory, which is, of course, palpably hollow. For indeed it is only by applying to the Bible a criticism, such as it is, that such a man makes out that criticism does not apply to the Bible.

There has grown up an irresistible sense that the belief in miracles was due to man's want of experience, to his ignorance, agitation and helplessness. And it will not do to stake all truth and value of the Bible upon its having been put out of the sky, upon its being guaranteed by miracles, and upon their being true. If we present the Bible in this fashion, then the cry *Imposture!* will more and more, in spite of all we can do, gather strength, and the book will be thrown aside more and more.

But when men come to see, that, both in the New Testament and in the Old, what is given us is words *thrown out* at an immense reality not fully or half fully grasped by the writers, but, even thus, able to affect us with indescribable force; when we convince ourselves that, as in the Old Testament we have

Israel's inadequate yet inexhaustibly fruitful testimony to *the Eternal that makes for righteousness,* so we have in the New Testament a report inadequate, indeed but the only report we have, and therefore priceless, by men, some more able and clear, others less able and clear, but *all* full of the influences of their time and condition, partakers of some of its simple or its learned ignorance, – inevitably, in fine, expecting miracles and demanding them, – a report, I say, by these men of that immense reality not fully or half fully grasped by them, *the mind of Christ,* – then we shall be drawn to the Gospels with a new zest and as by a fresh spell. We shall throw ourselves upon their narratives with an ardour answering to the value of the pearl of great price they hold, and to the difficulty of reaching it.

So, to profit fully by the New Testament, the first thing to be done is to make it perfectly clear to oneself that its reporters both could err and did err. For a plain person, an incident in the report of St Paul's conversion, – which comes into our minds the more naturally as this incident has been turned against something we ourselves said, – would, one would think, be enough. We had spoken of the notion that St Paul's miraculous vision at his conversion proved the truth of his doctrine. We related a vision which converted Sampson Staniforth, one of the early Methodists; and we said that just so much proving force, and no more, as Sampson Staniforth's vision had to confirm the truth of anything he might afterwards teach, St Paul's vision had to establish *his* subsequent doctrine. It was eagerly rejoined that Staniforth's vision was but a fancy of his own, whereas the reality of Paul's was proved by his companions hearing the voice that spoke to him. And so in one place of the Acts we are told they did; but in another place of the Acts we are told by Paul himself just the contrary: that his companions did *not* hear the voice that spoke to him. Need we say that the two statements have been 'reconciled'? They have, over and

over again; but by one of the processes which are the oppro-
brium of our Bible-criticism, and by which, as Bishop Butler
says, anything can be made to mean anything; There is between
the two statements a contradiction as clear as can be. The contradiction proves nothing against the good faith of the reporter,
and St Paul undoubtedly had his vision; he had it as Sampson
Staniforth had his. What the contradiction proves is the
incurable looseness with which the circumstances of what is
called and thought a miracle are related; and that this looseness
the Bible-relaters of *a miracle* exhibit, just like other people. And
the moral is: what an unsure stay, then, must miracles be!

. . .

And the more the miraculousness of the story deepens, as after
the death of Jesus, the more does the texture of the incidents
become loose and floating, the more does the very air and aspect
of things seem to tell us we are in wonderland. Jesus after his
resurrection not known by Mary Magdalene, taken by her for
the gardener; *appearing in another form*, and not known by the
two disciples going with him to Emmaus and at supper with
him there; not known by his most intimate apostles on the
borders of the Sea of Galilee; – and presently, out of these vague
beginnings, the recognitions getting asserted, then the ocular
demonstrations, the final commissions, the ascension; – one
hardly knows which of the two to call the most evident here,
the perfect simplicity and good faith of the narrators or the
plainness with which they themselves really say to us: *Behold
a legend growing under your eyes!*

And suggestions of this sort, with respect to the whole
miraculous side of the New Testament, will meet us at every
turn; we here but give a sample of them. It is neither our wish
nor our design to accumulate them, to marshal them, to insist
upon them, to make their force felt. Let those who desire to
keep them at arms length continue to do so, if they can, and

go on placing the sanction of the Christian religion in its miracles. Our point is, that the objections to miracles do, and more and more will, without insistence, without attack, without controversy, make their own force felt; and that the sanction of Christianity, if Christianity is not to be lost along with its miracles, must be found elsewhere.

MATTHEW ARNOLD
Literature and Dogma

As Exquisite as the Coming of Spring

Yet the whole life of Christ – so entirely may sorrow and beauty be made one in their meaning and manifestation – is really an idyll, though it ends with the veil of the temple being rent, and the darkness coming over the face of the earth, and stone rolled to the door of the sepulchre. One always thinks of him as a young bridegroom with his companions, as indeed he somewhere describes himself; as a shepherd straying through a valley with his sheep in search of green meadow or cool stream; as a singer trying to build out of the music the walls of the City of God; or as a lover for whose love the whole world was too small. His miracles seem to me to be as exquisite as the coming of spring, and quite as natural. I see no difficulty at all in believing that such was the charm of his personality that his mere presence could bring peace to souls in anguish, and that those who touched his garments or his hands forgot their pain; or that as he passed by on the highway of life people who had seen nothing of life's mystery saw it clearly, and others who had been deaf to every voice but that of pleasure heard for the first time the voice of love and found it as 'musical as Apollo's lute'; or that evil passions fled at his approach, and men whose dull unimaginative lives had been but a mode of death rose as it were from the grave when he called them; or that when he taught on the hillside the multitude forgot their hunger and thirst and the cares of this world, and that to his friends who listened to him as he sat at meat the coarse food seemed delicate, and the water had the taste of good wine, and the whole house became full of the odour and sweetness of nard.

OSCAR WILDE
De Profundis

―

Terrible Objection

To M. de Franquières

As for Jesus, the sublime flight of his great soul always raised him above every other mortal, and from the age of twelve until he expired in the cruellest, indeed the most infamous of all deaths, he never for one moment went back on his word. His noble plan was to lift up his people, to make them once more free and worthy to be so; for that was the way to begin. The profound study he made of the Law of Moses, his efforts to awaken love and enthusiasm for it in men's hearts, revealed his aim in so far as was possible without startling the Romans. But his vile and cowardly compatriots, instead of listening, took to hating him precisely because of his genius and virtue, which were a reproach to their baseness. In the end, it was only after realising the impossibility of carrying out his plan that, in his mind, he enlarged it, and that, unable on his own to cause a revolution among his People, he wished his disciples to cause one throughout the Universe. He was prevented from succeeding in his first plan, not only by the vileness of his people who were incapable of virtue, but by the too great gentleness of his own character; the gentleness of an angel or of God rather than of man, which never deserted him even on the cross and which causes tears to stream from the eyes of anyone who knows how to read his life properly, and see through the rubbish by which these poor people have distorted him. Fortunately they have respected and faithfully transcribed his speeches which they did not hear; take away a few eastern expressions or bad renderings, and not a word is unworthy of him, and it is here that you recognize the divine man who, despite their rough, proud enthusiasm, made eloquent and courageous men of his wretched disciples.

You reproach me with his miracles. Your objection would be terrible if it was justified. But you know, Monsieur, or at least you could know that, according to me, far from Jesus having done any miracles, he declared very positively that he would not do any, and showed the greatest disdain for those who demanded them.

JEAN-JACQUES ROUSSEAU
Lettres de la Montagne

Consolation Stories

Reading the New Testament provides a picture of Jesus with his loving prediliction for drawing close to men and women who were otherwise forsaken or held in contempt. In the villages around the lake were victims of malaria, whom healthy people despised for being possessed by an evil spirit, yet Jesus tended their needs. The lepers, forbidden to approach any village or town, were considered under the Law to be unclean and to be the recipients of punishment from God (Leviticus 13:1), yet Jesus ignored that part of the Law and tried to help them. He enlisted into his group of close disciples one of the tax collectors who were always objects of derision. Nor did he turn his nose up at the prostitutes, always the objects of public disdain.

The gospels have many stories about Jesus and these abandoned souls. The stories are of two kinds: one is where Jesus heals their infirmities by a miracle, what are termed 'miracle stories'; the other is where, rather than performing a miracle, Jesus simply shares with them their pitiable suffering – in other words, 'consolation stories'. Why is it then that, between the two, it is the consolation stories which carry a greater sense of reality than do the miracle stories? Why is it that the consolation stories are far more effective in portraying a lifelike picture of Jesus and in bringing vividly before our eyes the circumstances of the story?

The following narrative, for example, occurs in the seventh chapter of Luke, beginning with verse 36:

> One of the Pharisees invited him to a meal with him. He entered the home of the Pharisee and reclined on a couch; and without warning, a woman who was a scandal in the town (a harlot) came in. After making sure that he was at table in the home of the Pharisee, she brought with her an alabaster flask of perfume, took her stand behind him at his feet and wept. Yielding to an impulse, she rained her tears on his feet and wiped them with her hair.

On reading this passage we can close our eyes and envision the circumstances not explicitly recorded.

Perhaps the harlot in the story was an impoverished girl in Magdala or some such place. She gave herself to any man in order to stay alive, and the man sneeringly gave her money in return for the fun of toying with her while she lay motionless beside him, empty eyes staring open in the dark.

From whom did she hear about Jesus? How did she get the idea of going to him? It could be that she had heard about Jesus one night from a man who had bought her service. It might even be that she caught sight of Jesus from a distance while he was sitting, tired and quiet, by the edge of the lake. She certainly knew very little about the sort of person Jesus was. Only from his demeanour did she gather the inexpressible kindly attitude that was his. Here was a woman, seasoned to her own misery and the contempt of others, who could recognize by instinct the sort of person who has real kindness of heart.

Because the house where Jesus was at table belonged to a Pharisee, when the woman entered, the servants likely tried to prevent her. To the Pharisees she was only a lowly whore to whom they held themselves forbidden to give so much as the time of day. In the world of the Old Testament these females were often the target of vehement denunciation from the prophets. She must have therefore shaken loose from the servants, stepped into the dining room, and walked straight toward Jesus through the gauntlet of open-mouthed stares turning on her from everybody at the table.

She spoke nothing. In silence she looked intently on Jesus. Soon the tears that formed in her eyes began to overflow. The tears alone bespoke the sorrow she knew. 'She rained her tears on his feet.' The trenchant expression is enough to have us know how pitiably wretched she was feeling.

The tears told Jesus everything. He understood her being a public object of contempt through half of her life, eating her heart out in lonely misery. The tears were enough. Don't weep anymore. As for me, I understand how unhappy you have been.

Jesus responded with gentleness. The words he quietly spoke are among the most beautiful in all the Bible. 'Her sins, which are many, are forgiven, for she loved much.' *Whoever loves much will be forgiven much.*

A consolation story like this appeals to us far more vividly than do many of the miracle stories concerning Jesus. The words chosen convey the woman's sadness – 'She rained her tears on his feet' – and the gently spoken words of forgiveness – 'Whoever loves much will be forgiven much' – have a ring to them which never fails to stir our emotions.

I will cite another one of the consolation stories. Matthew, Mark and Luke each presents his own account of what happened with the woman who suffered from chronic bleeding of the uterus.

> There was in the crowd a woman who had a flow of blood for twelve years, and who had suffered much under many physicians, and had spent all she had, and was not better but rather grew worse. She had heard the reports about Jesus, and came up behind him in a crowd and touched his garment . . . Jesus said, 'Who touched my garment?' (Mark 5:25)

This event too occurred in a town by the lake of Galilee. The woman, mingling unobtrusively in the crowd that was pressing in to get a look at Jesus, had suffered so long from her incurable haemorraging that her act of touching a trembling finger to his clothing was like a drowning person catching at a straw. At merely the touch of this timid finger Jesus felt all the burden of her suffering and the desperation which made her grasp at straws.

'Who touched my clothes?' he said, turning to the disciples. They laughed, replying, 'You see the crowd pressing upon you and yet you ask, "Who touched me?" How can you avoid being jostled?'

'No, you're wrong,' said Jesus, shaking his head. 'Somebody has touched my clothing.'

Then among all the faces watching him, he distinguished the frightened look on one woman's face.

The story leads into the miracle story of how Jesus heals the woman's malady, but to me the affecting part is how Jesus felt all the woman's heartbreaking suffering through the touch of her trembling finger against his clothing – more moving than the sequel in which he cures her ailment with a miracle. The woman's finger reaches furtively from behind other people, and when it barely comes in contact with his outer garment, Jesus turns and understands her suffering. From the single trembling finger we complete the picture of the woman's frightened face and the heart-stricken look from the face of Jesus.

If the consolation stories seem more realistic than do the miracle stories, could the explanation be that the miracles of Jesus were put into writing only after the many oral traditions concerning Jesus had been collected from the back country towns of Galilee, in contrast to the other stories based on eyewitness accounts still fresh in the memory of the disciples themselves and written down with no embroidering?

SHUSAKU ENDO

A Life of Jesus

GOSPELS: TRUE OR FALSE?

As New as Newspaper Reports

Now the first thing to note is that if we take it merely as a human story, it is in some ways a very strange story. I do not refer here to its tremendous and tragic culmination or to any implications involving triumph in that tragedy. I do not refer to what is commonly called the miraculous element; for on that point philosophies vary and modern philosophies very decidedly waver. Indeed the educated Englishman of today may be said to have passed from an old fashion in which he would not believe in any miracles unless they were ancient, and adopted a new fashion in which he will not believe in any miracles unless they are modern. He used to hold that miraculous cures stopped with the first Christians and is now inclined to suspect that they began with the first Christian Scientists. But I refer here rather specially to unmiraculous and even to unnoticed and inconspicuous parts of the story. There are a great many things about it which nobody would have invented, for they are things that nobody has ever made any particular use of; things which if they were remarked at all have remained rather as puzzles. For instance, there is that long stretch of silence in the life of Christ up to the age of thirty. It is of all silences the most immense and imaginatively impressive. But it is not the sort of thing that anybody is particularly likely to invent in order to prove something and nobody so far as I know has ever tried to prove anything in particular from it. It is impressive, but it is only impressive as a fact; there is nothing particularly popular or obvious about making it a fable. The ordinary trend of hero-worship and myth-making is much more likely to say the precise opposite. It is much more likely to say (as I believe some of the gospels rejected by the Church do say) that Jesus displayed a divine precocity and began his mission at a miraculously early age. And there is indeed something strange in the thought that he who of all humanity needed least preparation seems to have had most. Whether it was some mode of the divine humility, or some truth of which we can see the shadow in the longer domestic tutelage of the higher creatures of the earth, I do not propose to speculate; I mention it simply as an example of the sort of thing that does in any case give rise to speculations. Now the whole story is full of these things. It is not by any means, as badly presented in print, a story that it is easy to get to the bottom of. It is anything but what these people talk of as a simple Gospel. Relatively speaking, it is the Gospel that has the mysticism and the Church that has the rationalism. As I should put it, of course, it is the Gospel that is the riddle and the Church that is the answer. But whatever the answer, the Gospel as it stands is almost a book of riddles.

First, a man reading the Gospel sayings would not find platitudes. If he had read even in the most respectful spirit the majority of ancient philosophers and of modern moralists, he would appreciate the unique importance of saying that he did not find platitudes. It is more than can be said even of Plato. It is much more than can be said of Epictetus or Seneca or Marcus Aurelius or Appollonius of Tyana. And it is immeasurably more than can be said of most of the agonistic moralists and the preachers of the ethical societies; with their songs of service and their religion of brotherhood. The morality of most moralists, ancient and modern, has been one solid and polished cataract of platitudes flowing forever and ever. That would certainly not be the impression of the imaginary independent outsider studying the New Testament. He would be conscious of nothing so commonplace and in a sense of nothing so continuous as that stream. He would find a number of strange claims that might sound like the claim to be the brother of the sun and moon; a number of very startling pieces of advice; a number of stunning rebukes; a number of strangely beautiful stories. He would see some very gigantesque figures of speech about the impossibility of threading a needle with a camel or the possibility of throwing a mountain into the sea. He would see a number of very daring simplifications of the difficulties of life; like the advice to shine upon everybody indifferently as does the sunshine or not to worry about the future any more than the birds. He would find on the other hand some passages of almost impenetrable darkness, so far as he is concerned such as the moral of the parable of the Unjust Steward. Some of these things might strike him as fables and some as truths; but none as truisms. For instance, he would not find the ordinary platitudes in favour of peace. He would find several paradoxes in favour of peace. He would find several ideals of non-resistance, which taken as they stand would be rather too pacific for any pacifist. He would be told in one passage to treat a robber *not* with passive resistance, but rather with positive and enthusiastic encouragement, if the terms be taken literally; heaping up gifts upon the man who had stolen goods. But he would not find a word of all that obvious rhetoric against a war which has filled countless books and odes and orations; not a word about the wickedness of war, the wastefulness of war, the appalling scale of the slaughter in war and all the rest of the familiar frenzy; indeed not a word about war at all. There is nothing that throws any particular light on Christ's attitude towards organised warfare, except that he seems to have been rather fond of Roman soldiers. Indeed it is another perplexity, speaking from the same external and human standpoint, that he seems to have got on much better with Romans than he did with Jews. But the question here is a certain tone to be appreciated by merely reading a certain text; and we might give any number of instances of it.

. . .

But the point here is that if we *could* read the Gospel reports as things as new as newspaper reports, they would puzzle us and perhaps terrify us much *more* than the same things as developed by historical Christianity. For instance: Christ, after a clear allusion to the eunuchs of eastern courts, said there would be eunuchs of the kingdom of heaven. If this does not mean the voluntary enthusiasm of virginity, it could be made to mean something much more unnatural or uncouth. It is the historical religion that humanises it for us by the experience of Franciscans or of Sisters of Mercy. The mere statement standing by itself might very well suggest a rather dehumanised atmosphere; the sinister and inhuman silence of the Asiatic harem and divan. This but one instance out of scores; but the moral is that the Christ of the Gospel might actually seem more strange and terrible than the Christ of the Church.

I am dwelling on the dark or dazzling or defiant or mysterious side of the Gospel words, not because they had not obviously a more obvious and popular side, but because this is the answer to a common criticism on a vital point. The freethinker frequently says that Jesus of Nazareth was a man of his time, even if he was in advance of his time; and that we cannot accept his ethics as final for humanity. The freethinker then goes on to criticise his ethics, saying plausibly enough that men cannot turn the other cheek, or that they must take thought for the morrow, or that the self-denial is too ascetic or the monogamy too severe. But the Zealots and the Legionaries did not turn the other cheek any more than we do, if so much. The Jewish traders and Roman tax-gatherers took thought for the morrow as much as we, if not more. We cannot pretend to be abandoning the morality of the past for one more suited to the present. It is certainly not the morality of another age, but it might be of another world.

In short, we can say that these ideals are impossible in themselves. Exactly what we cannot say is that they are impossible for us. They are rather notably marked by a mysticism which, if it be a sort of madness, would always have struck the same sort of people as mad. Take, for instance, the case of marriage and the relations of the sexes. It might very well have been true that a Galilean teacher taught things more natural to a Galilean environment; but it is not. It might rationally be accepted that a man in the time of Tiberius would have advanced a view conditioned by the time of Tiberius; but he did not. What he advanced was something quite different; something very difficult; but something no more difficult now than it was then. When, for instance Mahomet made his polygamous compromise we may reasonably say that it was conditioned by a polygamous society. When he allowed a man four wives he was really doing something suited to the circumstances, which might have been less suited to other circumstances. Nobody will pretend that the four wives were like the four winds, something seemingly a part of the order of nature; nobody will say that the figure four was written forever in stars upon the sky. But neither will anyone say that the figure four is an inconceivable ideal; that it is beyond the power of the mind of man to count up to four; or to count the number of his wives and see if it amounts to four. It is a practical compromise carrying with it the character of a particular society. If Mahomet had been born in Acton in the nineteenth century, we may well doubt whether he would instantly have filled that suburb with harems of four wives apiece. As he was born in Arabia in the sixth century, he did in his conjugal arrangements suggest the conditions of Arabia in the sixth century. But Christ in his view of marriage does not in the least suggest the conditions of Palestine in the first century. He does not suggest anything at all, except the sacramental view of marriage as developed long afterwards by the Catholic Church. It was quite as difficult for people then as it is for people now. It was much more puzzling to people then than to people now. Jews and Romans and Greeks did not believe, and did not even understand enough to disbelieve, the mystical idea that the man and the woman had become one sacramental substance. We may think it an incredible or impossible ideal; but we cannot think it any more incredible or impossible than they would have thought it. In other words, whatever else is true, it is not true that the controversy has been altered by time. Whatever else is true, it is emphatically not true that the ideas of Jesus of Nazareth were suitable to his time, but are no longer suitable to our time. Exactly how suitable they were to his time is perhaps suggested in the end of his story.

The same truth might be stated in another way by saying that if the story be regarded as merely human and historical, it is extraordinary how very little there is in the recorded words of Christ that ties him at all to his own time. I do not mean the details of a period, which even a man of the period knows to be passing. I mean the fundamentals which even the wisest man often vaguely assumes to be eternal. For instance, Aristotle was perhaps the wisest and most wide-minded man who ever lived. He founded himself entirely upon fundamentals, which have been generally found to remain rational and solid through all social and historical changes. Still, he lived in a world in which it was thought as natural to have slaves as to have children. And therefore he did permit himself a serious recognition of a difference between slaves and free men. Christ as much as Aristotle lived in a world that took slavery for granted. He did not particularly denounce slavery. But he started a movement that could exist in a world without slavery. He never used a phrase that made his philosophy depend even upon the very existence of the social order in which he lived. He spoke as one conscious that everything was ephemeral, including the things that Aristotle thought eternal. By that time the Roman Empire had come to be merely the orbis terrarum, another name for the world. But he never made his morality dependent on the existence of the Roman Empire or even on the existence of the world. 'Heaven and earth shall pass away; but my words shall not pass away.'

G.K. CHESTERTON
The Essential G.K. Chesterton

You Couldn't Make Him Up

If it was proved he never existed then the invention would reflect huge credit on the human race for having had the most extraordinary idea in its history. It would take soaring genius to make Him up. He could not have been worked out by a committee. The pagan gods are pitifully dull and predictable in comparison with His strangeness. I don't believe the human race is capable of such invention – not on the evidence. Rather than having created Him they try to diminish Him to match themselves.

ALICE THOMAS ELLIS
from the author's journal

A Personality

There are learned men who deny that Jesus called the Christ is an historic figure; that such a man ever lived and died on earth. I have considered their arguments, but cannot accept them, and for special reason: that, as a student and creator of fiction, I recognize, or believe that I recognize in the Gospel narratives the presence of a personality. I meet there a man of loving-kindness, and at the same time of energy and passion; a man hating injustice and fighting for righteousness. Such a personality cannot have come into existence by accident, or by the accumulation of any number of Orphic and Mithraic and Egyptian sun-god myths.

UPTON SINCLAIR
A Personal Jesus

Eye-witness

The Twentieth chapter of St John's Gospel can stand with the best eye-witness reports.

GRAHAM GREENE
M.F. Allain, *The Other Man*

The Cunning of the Evangelists

Easter Sunday [1844].

Evidences of art in Bible narratives. They are written with a watchful attention (though disguised) as to their effect on the reader. Their so-called simplicity is, in fact, the simplicity of the highest cunning. And one is led to inquire, when even in these latter days artistic development and arrangement are the qualities least appreciated by readers, who was there likely to appreciate the art in these chronicles at that day?

Looking round on a well-selected shelf of fiction or history, how few stories of any length does one recognize as well told from beginning to end! The first half of this story, the last half of that, the middle of another . . . The modern art of narration is yet in its infancy.

But in these Bible lives and adventures there is the spherical completeness of perfect art. And our first, and second, feeling that they must be true because they are so impressive, becomes, as a third feeling, modified to, 'Are they so very true, after all?' Is not the fact of their being so convincing, an argument, not for their actuality, but for the actuality of a consummate artist who was no more content with what Nature offered than Sophocles and Pheidias were content?'

THOMAS HARDY

M. Millgate, *The Life and Works of Thomas Hardy*

Amazement Prevails

The threat of hell seems especially vivid in Matthew, and ready to hand, to brandish as a menace: in two separate places (5: 29–30; 18:8–9) he repeats the ferocious admonishment found in Mark 9:43–48:

> If your hand leads you into evil, cut it off: it is better for you to come into Life maimed than, with both hands, to depart into hell, into the fire that cannot be put out. And if your foot leads you into evil, cut it off: it is better for you to come into Life crippled than, with both feet, to be cast into hell. And if your eye leads you into evil, pluck it out: it is better for you to come into the Kingdom of God with one eye than, with two, to be cast into hell, where their worm does not die and the fire is never quenched.

These are among the hardest of the not unnumerous hard sayings of Jesus, and Matthew brings them to the fore; his presentation delights in a moral perfectionism. 'You then must be perfect, as your Father in Heaven is perfect' (5:48). The Kingdom of Heaven is very precarious of entrance, a matter of jots and tittles of the ancient Law: 'The man who abolishes one of these little rules and teaches people to forget it shall count for little in the Kingdom of Heaven' (5:19).

What is this Kingdom of Heaven? At times it seems to be a revolutionized earth, an earth brought under the rule of God; at others a realm of an otherworldly afterlife, the opposite of hell and outer darkness. And yet again it seems a new state of inner being, a state of moral perfection that is not so much the ticket to the Kingdom but the Kingdom itself. In Luke, Jesus tells his disciples, 'Watch as you may, you will not see it come. People will not be saying "Here it is!" or "There!" And the reason why is this – this Kingdom of God is within you' (17:20–21). The most extended statement concerning the Kingdom, and the longest compilation of Christ's instruction, comes in Matthew, Chapters 5 through 7, and it is this so-called Sermon on the Mount, or Great Instruction, that would be the sorest loss if Matthew's Gospel, in that precarious welter of first-century Christian testimony, had vanished along with Q and Matthew's supposed version in Hebrew. Luke's shorter version of the Sermon, delivered not on a mountain but on a plain, in 6: 17–49, is less than half as long, and strikes a merry note peculiar to itself: 'Happy, you that weep now; for you shall laugh.' Matthew does not mention laughing, but his extended collection of the sayings of Jesus holds many touches of that sublime gallantry, that cosmic carefreeness which emanates from the Son of Man:

> Count yourselves happy when the time comes for people to revile you and maltreat you and utter every kind of calumny against you on account of me.

Let your light so shine upon the world that it may see the beauty of your life and give glory to your Father in Heaven.

If anyone strikes you on the right cheek, turn the left towards him also. If anyone sees fit to sue you for your tunic, let him have your cloak as well. If anyone impresses you to go a mile, go along with him for two.

Love your enemies and pray to those that persecute you, so that you may become children of your Father in Heaven, who causes his sun to rise on the wicked and the good, and rains on the just and the unjust alike.

Do not amass for yourselves treasure on earth, where moth and rust destroy, and thieves break in and steal.

Learn from the lilies of the fields and how they grow. They do not work, they do not spin. But I tell you that not even Solomon in all his glory was robed like one of these.

Do not judge, lest you be judged.

Do not give holy things to dogs, nor scatter your pearls in front of swine, or they may trample them underfoot, and turn and tear you to pieces.

Ask and you shall receive. Seek and you shall find. Knock and the door shall be opened to you. For everyone that asks receives; every seeker finds; and to everyone that knocks the door is opened.

These commands do not form a prescription for life in this world. The auditors are described as 'filled with amazement at his teaching; for he taught them like one with authority not like the Doctors who usually taught them.' The concept of amazement recurs in this part of Matthew. In the next chapter, the disciples are, in Rieu's translation, 'amazed' at Jesus's stilling the wind and sea, and Jesus is 'amazed' at the faith of the centurion who comes to Jesus to heal his paralyzed son.

The worlds are colliding; amazement prevails. Jesus's healing and preaching go together in the Gospel accounts, and his preaching is healing of a sort, for it banishes worldly anxiety; it overthrows the common-sense and materially verifiable rules that, like the money-changers in the Temple, dominate the world with their practicality. Jesus declares an inversion of the world's order, whereby the first shall be last and the last first, the meek shall inherit the earth, the hungry and thirsty shall be satisfied, and the poor in spirit shall possess the Kingdom of Heaven. This Kingdom is the hope and pain of Christianity; it is attained against the grain, through the denial of instinctive and social wisdom and through faith in the unseen. Using natural metaphors as effortlessly as an author quoting his own works, Jesus disclaims nature and its rules of survival. Nature's way, obvious and broad, leads to death; this other way is narrow and difficult: 'Come in by the narrow gate, for the way to destruction is a broad and open road which is trodden by many; whereas the way to life is by a narrow gate and a difficult road, and few are those that find it' (7: 13–14).

Life is not what we think and feel it is. True life (sometimes capitalized 'Life' in Rieu's translation, as in the quotation from Mark above) is something different to the life of the body: 'He that wins his life will lose it, and he that loses his life for my sake shall win it' (10:39). Christ's preaching threatens men, the virtuous even more than the wicked, with a radical transformation of value whereby the rich and pious are damned and harlots and tax-collectors are rather more acceptable. The poor, ignorant, and childish are more acceptable yet: Jesus thanks God 'for hiding these things from wise and clever men and revealing them to simple folk' (11:25). Even ordinary altruism is challenged, and decent frugality, in the incident of the woman who poured precious ointment over Jesus, to the amazement and indignation of the apostles. They object, 'That might have fetched a good price, and so been given to the poor.' The blithe, deathless answer is given: 'You have the poor among your always; but me you have not always' (26:11). Over against human perspective stands God's perspective, from which even sparrows sold two for a farthing have value. Just so, each human soul, including those of women and slaves and gentiles, has value. From our perspective, the path of righteousness is narrow; but the strait gate leads to infinite consolation: 'Put on my yoke and learn from me, who am gentle and humble in heart – and you will find rest for your souls. For my yoke is easy and my burden light' (11:28–30). Fulfillment of the old Law turns out to be close to lawlessness; circumcision, dietary restrictions, strict observance of the Sabbath, familial piety, Pharisaical scruples are all swept away the new dispensation. Said John the Baptist: 'He will baptize you in the Holy Spirit and fire. His winnowing-fan is in his hand. He will clear his threshing-floor and gather the grain into his barn' (3:11–12). Said Jesus: 'The blind see once more; the lame walk; lepers are cleansed; the deaf hear; dead men are brought back to life, and beggars are proclaiming the Good News. Happy the man who finds no fault in me' (11:5–6).

JOHN UPDIKE
'St Matthew's Gospel' from *Odd Jobs*

Stern Test

Perhaps the most distinctive and haunting of all Matthew's stories – perhaps the most haunting passage in the entire New Testament – is that parable in the final discourse (25: 32–46) when Jesus predicts that the King will welcome the chosen into his kingdom. They are those who have seen him, not in his glory, but as poor, naked, hungry, in prison and in need. Neither the blessed, nor the damned, in this tale, understand during their lifetimes, that in so far as they responded to the depths of human need in others, they had responded to God. It is in the context of this story that we begin to understand the sense in which this book is true. By the stern test of that parable and of this Gospel, most of us will feel like that rich young man. We will go away sorrowful, deeply conscious of our inability either to understand the Gospel, or to live up to its precepts or to have the humility to accept Divine Grace. Yet, though we are sorrowful, and though we go away, we shall never read this text without being, in some small degree, changed.

A.N. WILSON
Introduction to *St Matthew's Gospel*

Self-Evident Sublimity

. . . Jesus Christ whose sublimity is self-evident to anyone who reads the Gospels with head unturned by the clap-trap of 'education' or perceptions undulled by some sentimental or stupid presentation.

KATHLEEN RAINE
Farewell Happy Fields

Drivelling Folly

It cannot be precisely ascertained [in] what degree Jesus Christ accommodated his doctrines to the opinions of his auditors, or in what degree he really said all that he is related to have said. He has left no written record of himself and we are compelled to judge from the imperfect and obscure information which his biographers, persons certainly of very undisciplined and undiscriminating minds, have transmitted to posterity. These writers, our only guides, impute sentiments to Jesus Christ which flatly contradict each other. The represent him as narrow, superstitious or exquisitely vindictive and malicious. They insert in the midst of a strain of impassioned eloquence, or

sagest exhortation, a sentiment only remarkable for its naked
and drivelling folly. But it is not difficult to distinguish the
inventions by which these historians have filled up the inters-
tices of tradition, or corrupted the simplicity of truth, from the
real character of the object of their rude amazement. They have
left sufficiently clear indications of the genuine character of
Jesus Christ to rescue it forever from the imputations cast upon
it by their ignorance and fanaticism. We discover that he is the
enemy of oppression and of falsehood, that he is the advocate of
equal justice, that he is neither disposed to sanction bloodshed or
deceit under whatsoever pretences their practice may be vindicated. We discover that he was a man of meek and majestic
demeanor, calm in danger, of natural and simple thought and
habits, beloved to adoration by his adherents, unmoved and
solemn and serene. It is utterly incredible that this man said
that if you hated your enemy you would find it to your account
to return him good for evil, since by such temporary oblivion
of vengeance you would heap coals of fire upon his head. Where
such contradictions occur, a favorable construction is warranted
by the general innocence of manners and comprehensiveness
of views which he is represented to possess.

The rule of criticism to be adopted in judging of the life,
actions, and words of a man who has acted any conspicuous
part in the revolutions of the world should not be narrow. We
ought to form a general image of his character and of his doctrines, and refer to this whole the distinct portions of actions
and of speech by which they are diversified. It is not here
asserted that no contradictions are to be admitted to have a
place in the system of Jesus Christ, between doctrines promul-
gated in different states of feeling or information, or even such
as are implied in the enunciation of a scheme of thought various
and obscure through its immensity and depth. It is not asserted
that no degree of human indignation ever hurried him beyond

the limits which his calmer mood had placed to disapprobation against vice and folly. Those deviations from the history of his life are alone to be vindicated which represent his own essential character in contradiction with itself. Every human mind has what Lord Bacon calls its *idola specus*, peculiar images which reside in the inner cave of thought. These constitute the essential and distinctive character of every human being, to which every action and every word bears intimate relation, and by which in depicting a character the genuineness and meaning of those words and actions are to be determined. Every fanatic or enemy of virtue is not at liberty to misrepresent the greatest geniuses and the most heroic defenders of all that is valuable in this mortal world. His story to gain any credit must contain some truth, and that truth shall thus be made a sufficient indication of his prejudice and his deceit.

With respect to the miracles which these biographers have related, I have already declined to enter into any discussion on their nature or their existence. The supposition of their false-hood or their truth would modify in no degree the hues of the picture which is attempted to be delineated. To judge truly of the moral and philosophical character of Socrates it is not necessary to determine the question of the familiar Spirit which it is supposed that he believed to attend him. The power of the human mind relatively to intercourse with or dominion over the invisible world is doubtless an interesting theme of dis-cussion, but the connection of the instance of Jesus Christ with the established religion of the country in which I write renders it dangerous to subject oneself to the imputation of introducing new gods or abolishing old ones, nor is the duty of mutual forbearance sufficiently understood to render it certain that the metaphysician and the moralist, even though he carefully sacri-fice a cock to Esculapius, may not receive something analogous to the bowl of hemlock for the reward of his labours.

Much however, of what his biographers have asserted is not to be rejected merely because of inferences inconsistent with the general spirit of his system are to be deduced from its admission. Jesus Christ did what every other reformer who has produced any considerable effect upon the world has done. He accommodated his doctrines to the prepossessions of those whom he addressed. He used a language for this view sufficiently familiar to our comprehensions. He said, however new or strange my doctrines may appear to you, they are, in fact only the restoration and re-establishment of those original institutions and ancient customs of your own law and religion. The constitution of your faith and policy, although perfect in their origin, have become corrupt and altered, and have fallen into decay. I profess to restore them to their pristine authority and splendor. 'Think not that I am come to destroy the law and the prophets. I am not come to destroy but to fulfill. Til Heaven and Earth shall pass away, one jot or one title shall in no wise pass from the Law till all be fulfilled.' [Misquotes Matt. 5.17–18]. Thus like a skilful orator (see Cicero's *De Oratore*), he secures the prejudices of his auditors and induces them by his professions of sympathy with their feelings to enter with a willing mind into the exposition of his own. The art of persuasion differs from that of reasoning, and it is of no small moment to the success even of a true cause that the judges who are to determine on its merits should be free from those national and religious predilections which render the multitude both deaf and blind. Let not this practice be considered as unworthy artifice. It were best for the cause of reason that mankind should acknowledge no authority but its own, but it is useful to a certain extent that they should not consider those institutions which they have been habituated to reverence as opposing an obstacle to its admission. All reformers have been compelled to practice this misrepresentation of their own true feelings and opinions. It is deeply to be lamented that a word should ever issue from human lips which contains the minutest alloy of dissimulation, or simulation, or hypocrisy, or exaggeration, or anything but the precise and rigid image which is present to the mind and which ought to dictate the expression. But this practice of entire sincerity towards other men would avail to no good end, if they were incapable of practicing it towards their own minds. In fact, truth cannot be communicated until it is perceived. The interests, therefore, of truth required that an orator should so far as possible produce in his hearers that state of mind in which alone his exhortations could fairly be contemplated and examined.

Having produced this favorable disposition of mind Jesus Christ proceeds to qualify and finally to abrogate the system of the Jewish Law. He descants upon insufficiency as a code of moral conduct, which it professed to be, and absolutely selects the law of retaliation as an instance of the absurdity and immorality of its institutions. The conclusion of the speech is in a strain of the most daring and most impassioned speculation. He seems emboldened by the success of his exculpation to the multitude to declare in public the utmost singularity of his faith. He tramples upon all received opinions, on all the cherished luxuries and superstitions of mankind. He bids them cast aside the chains of custom and blind faith by which they have been encompassed from the very cradle of their being, and become the imitators and ministers of the Universal God.

PERCY BYSSHE SHELLEY
Shelley's Prose

Somewhat Anti-Semitic

The Gospels are somewhat anti-semitic in tendency. I might paraphrase Dr Rouse: This is the story of a man who set out to reform Jewry from the inside, and they did not like it.

EZRA POUND
A Guide to Kulchur

A Man of Unusual Learning

Jesus was a man of unusual learning, wit and piety; his chief sponsors were members of the religious aristocracy of Jerusalem; and under the synagogue system then in force the general educational level of the Jewish artisan class, from which most of the disciples seem to have been drawn, was higher than that of any other in the world, the Greek included. All available evidence goes to show that the original Nazarene Gospel was terse, factually accurate and intellectually satisfying to those students of the law and the prophets for whom it was primarily intended. But Gentile heretics pirated it, mistranslated it into pedestrian Greek, recast it, and then subjected it to a century-long process of emendation and manipulation. The glamour of the early Jacobean prose in which the Gospels are now clothed, and their judicial authority, are most deceptive. Judged by Greek literary standards, they are poor; by historical standards, unreliable; and their doctrine is confused and contradictory. The late-Victorian atheist (was it Bradlaugh?) may be excused for remarking that they read as though 'concocted by illiterate, half-starved visionaries in some dark corner of a Graeco-Syrian slum.'

ROBERT GRAVES
The Nazarene Gospel Restored

The Extraordinary Fact of Jesus

The Christian Church has the great initial advantage over others in possessing the extraordinary fact of Jesus. Even if he never existed he would still be a great fact – the repository in which is held, the image in which is enshrined, the highest ideals of Man. But we do not have to take that view. 'And Jesus went before them: and they were amazed; and as they followed, they were afraid.' Obviously that was not invented; it was a simple report of an experience of awe of a phenomenon which was amazing, and which was so powerful in effect that Christianity could grow from it. We today can still open ourselves to a contemplation of that phenomenon or numen or whatever term we need, and enrich our spiritual awareness. It is not too difficult to do this since the New Testament is such a striking achievement and so soaked in numinous feeling – that is, so long as we do not use modernized versions which, evidently composed by unreligious clerics and unliterary scholars, eliminate the most important elements.

JOHN STEWART COLLIS
Bound Upon a Course

The Ring of Truth

I am a fairly versatile man of letters. I have been almost every sort of journalist from a crime reporter to a dramatic critic, from a gossip writer to an editor of a magazine. I have published novels, essays, autobiographies, pamphlets, produced plays, revues, etc. etc. All these things may be, and probably are, ephemeral and without merit. That is not the point. The point is that it is hardly possible for a man who has had so much traffic with the written and the spoken word to avoid attaining a certain competence in judging the true word from the false.

Let me make this point clearer by analogy. Certain learned judges, who over a period of many years have listened to the cross-examination of witnesses, acquire, after a time, a sort of sixth sense. 'That woman is lying', they say to themselves, and often, I have no doubt, they would find it difficult to explain exactly why they knew she was lying – they would only know that their mind was full of the echoes of past crimes and ancient falsehoods and half-forgotten treacheries, and that this woman's voice rang down that same dark gallery of liars.

Now this sixth sense is also bestowed, I believe, on those whose business it has been, over any considerable period, to sift the true from the false in literature. Consider the journalist. Any decent journalist – and there are lots of them drinking far too many double whiskies over the bars of Fleet Street – will be able to tell you, with absolute authority, when a story is faked and when it isn't. The general public may be deceived. They may think that Mr X's weekly article on Mothers is too touching, whereas the journalist may know that Mr X writes his article with his left hand and beats his mother with his right. The general public may think Lord Y's stirring call to England's youth really comes from the heart, whereas the little man in Fleet Street knows that as soon as Lord Y had written it he rang up his broker, sold a block of War Loan, bought Japanese industrials with the proceeds, and then went off to stay with a German blonde in the South of France. You can't fool Fleet Street. Sometimes I wish you could.

And I speak as a hard-bitten man of Fleet Street when I say that some of the Resurrection stories have an apparently unmistakable ring of truth. I say 'apparently' unmistakable because we can all tell stories of men and women who have uttered black lies to us while the light of truth and friendship shone on their faces. But no liar I have ever met in this world or ever hope to meet in the next was as good a liar as St

John when he told the story of how Christ appeared to Mary Magdalene.

You remember how it happened? She had visited the tomb. They had said to her, 'Woman, why weepest thou?'

'She saith unto them, Because they have taken away my Lord, and I know not where they have laid him. And when she had said thus, she turned herself back, and saw Jesus standing, and knew not that it was Jesus. Jesus saith unto her, Woman why weepest thou? Whom seekest thou? She, supposing him to be the gardener, saith unto him, Sir, if thou have borne him hence, tell me where thou hast laid him, and I will take him away. Jesus saith unto her, Mary. She turned herself, and saith unto him, Rabboni; which is to say, Master.'

Those two gentle words.

The gentle 'Mary', echoing in the garden.

The breathless 'Master', as she saw his face.

If we believe that story, it is one of the loveliest things that the printed word will ever give us. It is a story over which, without shame, a man may weep.

If we do not believe it, it is a brilliant but shameful lie.

Does it sound like that to you?

Does it sound fake?

'Jesus saith unto her, Mary. She turned herself, and saith unto him, Rabboni, which is to say, Master.'

BEVERLEY NICHOLS
The Fool Hath Said

Mark as Good as Maupassant

On finishing the Old Testament, before beginning the New, the reader stands, if I may borrow a simile from Keats, like a traveller on a peak in Darien, an ocean on either hand; oceans of storm and peace difficult to reconcile.

It is not possible that anybody in these islands could bring a virgin mind to the Bible, least of all to the Gospels, and my intellectual virginity was, after all, only relative. I had heard that everybody was agreed that the Gospel of John was merely an ecclesiastical work written about two centuries after the death of Christ; and I had heard that Luke was the man of letters; and having perforce to begin with one it seemed to me that I might as well begin with Luke as with another. I think I was disappointed almost from the first. A great weariness certainly overtook me about the middle of his narrative, and King Solomon's saying that 'there is no end to the making of books' came up in my mind, and I said: 'A polished, lifeless narrative written by a skilful man of letters, sleek as Maeterlinck;' for Maeterlinck is a very skilful and elaborate writer who knows how to burnish his prose, so that it shall seem like poetry to the ignorant. And what I miss in the Belgian I miss also in Luke – the essential. In Luke's narrative Christ seems a lifeless, waxen figure, daintily curled, with tinted cheeks, uttering pretty commonplaces gathered from The Treasure of the Lowly as he goes by. The Gospel of Matthew I liked a great deal better; Christ attains to some reality in it, despite a certain retouching of the text. 'A canvas that has passed,' I said, 'through the hands of the restorer.' The verses in which Christ gives Peter the keys of the kingdom of heaven, saying: 'Thou art Peter, and upon this rock I will build my church; and the gates of hell shall not prevail against it, and whatsoever thou shalt bind on earth shall be bound in heaven, and whatsoever thou shalt loose on earth shall be loosed in heaven,' are easily recognised by the critical mind as ecclesiastical paint. Remembering that I had heard somewhere, 'Whosoever's sins ye remit they are remitted unto them; and whosoever's sins ye retain they are retained,' I turned up the passage in John, and could not help smiling at the deftness with which the ecclesiastical reviser had improved upon his predecessor; and the thought popped up that, while inditing this emendation, the writer of the fourth Gospel had had his eye on my poor country, for in Ireland purgatory yields richer dividends than any other commercial enterprise, whether brewery or distillery.

It was not until I turned to the Gospel of Mark that I caught a glimpse of the real Christ, the magnificent young heretic who came up from Galilee to overthrow the priests in Jerusalem. How far the story told by Mark is true in fact we shall never know, but it is certain that it is true upon paper. That excellent chronicler wrote with his eyes on the scenes he describes, though he may not have been eye-witness to them; and his narrative reveals the same qualities that we admire in Maupassant. He is as concise, as explicit and as objective. I doubt if a story was ever better told; we get the legend (a legend is any story that has been passed from mouth to mouth, therefore a legend may be created in six days as well as sixty years) in Mark in its folk simplicity, as it was related some sixty years after the Crucifixion. An admirable narrative without ecclesiastical introduction, the story beginning as the Frenchman would have begun it: John baptizing a great multitude in the Jordan, Jesus coming to him for baptism which he receives, forthwith retiring into the desert, and coming out of it forty days after to preach in Galilee.

The narrative is strict throughout, and it seems to me the one Gospel of any historical value.

GEORGE MOORE
'On Reading the Bible for the First Time'

A Garden of Lilies

Of late I have been studying with diligence the four prose poems about Christ. At Christmas I managed to get hold of a Greek Testament and every morning, after I had cleaned my cell and polished my tins, I read a little of the Gospels, a dozen verses taken by chance anywhere. It is a delightful way of opening the day. Everyone, even in a turbulent, ill-disciplined life, should do the same. Endless repetition, in and out of season, has spoiled for us the freshness, the naivete, the too simple romantic charm of the Gospels. We hear them read far too often and far too badly, and all repetition is anti-spiritual. When one returns to the Greek, it is like going into a garden of lilies out of some narrow and dark house.

And to me, the pleasure doubled by the reflection that it is extremely probable that we have the actual terms, the *ipsissima verba*, used by Christ. It was always supposed that Christ talked in Aramaic. Even Renan thought so. But now we know that the Galilean peasants, like the Irish peasants of our own day, were bilingual, and that Greek was the ordinary language of intercourse all over Palestine, as indeed all over the Eastern world. I never liked the idea that we knew of Christ's own words only through a translation of a translation. It is a delight to me to think that as far as his conversation was concerned, Charmides might have listened to him, and Socrates reasoned with him, and Plato understood him: that he really said ἐγώ εἰμι ὁ ποιμὴν ὁ καλός, *that when he thought of the lilies of the field and how they neither toil nor spin, his absolute expression was* καταμάθετε τὰ κρίνα τοῦ ἀγροῦ πῶς αἰξάνεν οὐ κοπιᾶ, οἴζὲ ηίθα, *and that his last word when he cried out 'my life has been completed, has reached its fulfilment, has been perfected', was exactly as St John tells us it was* τετέλεσται—*no more.*

While in reading the Gospels – particularly that of St John himself, or whatever early Gnostic took his name and mantle – I see the continual assertion of the imagination as the basis of all spiritual and material life, I see also that to Christ imagination was simply a form of love, and that to him love was lord in the fullest meaning of the phrase. Some six weeks ago I was allowed by the doctor to have white bread to eat instead of the coarse black or brown bread of ordinary prison fare. It is a great delicacy. It will sound strange that dry bread could possible be a delicacy to anyone To me it is so much so that the close of each meal I carefully eat whatever crumbs may be left on my tin plate, or have fallen on the rough towel that one uses as a cloth so as not to soil one's table; and I do so not from hunger – I get now quite sufficient food – but simply in order that nothing should be wasted of what is given to me. So one should look on love.

OSCAR WILDE

De Profundis

Simplicity

The beauty of the Bible is that the most Ignorant and Simple Minds Understand it Best.

WILLIAM BLAKE

Annotations on Dr Thornton's Translation of the Lord's Prayer

A Drama Equal to the Greek Plays

Let us pretend for a moment, reader, that you are literally, and not merely metaphorically, a book-worm, a book-worm endowed with superhuman curiosity, who, in some huge terrestrial Bodleian, has nibbled at the 'logoi' of Lao-Tze and Kwang-Tze, at the 'logoi' of Buddha and Zoroaster, a real book-worm, more innocent of the actual world than the greatest scholar. What would such a devourer of Great Men make of this biography of Jesus as the artful poet-doctor* rounds it off for the benefit of Theophilus?

*St Luke.

He would be quite ignorant, let us remember, of the disputes of Catholics and Protestants, of Rationalists and Religionists. he would not 'even so much as have heard' that there was an Archbishop of Canterbury. All he would know about Jesus, and about this 'Kingdom' of his, would be what St Luke tells him – no more and no less. It would be King James's Version he would be devouring; and as he moved from page to page of that strange itinerary, with Jerusalem ever growing always nearer, and the as-yet-untenanted tomb of the Arimathean growing always nearer, he would, I think, cry out that he had found a drama equal to all the Greek plays put together. Ignorant of so much as he would have been, he would at least, in his vermicular progress through the library of Theophilus, know what physical pain meant and what necessity meant, and what shame and remorse and humiliation meant, and what pride and hypocrisy and self-righteousness meant. Above all, he would know, what every worm knows, whether born in the leaves of a Bible or in the wood of a Gallows, that there's some illness, some sickness, some curse upon life, that makes cheerful endurance rather than thrilling happiness the prevailing temper of organic creation.

And our vermicular pilgrim would be surprised to discover that the *phenomenon of pain*, whether physical or mental, was not here, as it was with Buddha, the crux, pivot, and chief motive-force of all philosophizing. He would soon become aware that pain for the children of the 'Kingdom' was incidental to life, was a means to life; and instead of 'Nirvana', or escape from the Great Wheel, what 'My Father's Kingdom' offered was simply 'more life,' life more abundant than ear has heard, or eye seen, or heart dared to imagine!

And he would further discover – with less of a shock, perhaps, *being what he was*, than if he'd been the body-louse of a Lama – that to be the lowest rather than the highest, the slave rather than the master, the fool rather than the wise, the last rather than the first, the tramp rather than the statesman, the harlot rather than the matriarch, the failure rather than the success, the abject rather than the distinguished, the desperate rather than the competent, was, though no more than pain and suffering, an end in itself, in fuller harmony with the spirit of the 'Kingdom' and offering a better chance of the 'life everlasting.'

Our book-worm would also be amazed, and even perhaps, if he were a very scholarly worm, a little horrified, at the part played by women in St Luke's Life of Jesus. Unused it may be to *quite* such *equality of all souls*, our little friend would find the 'tempo' of this biography to savour more of the cheaper daily papers than the *Education of Henry Adams*. Women and marvels, Love and marvels, Wedding-Feasts and marvels, Madmen and marvels, Obstruction of Traffic and marvels, Faith-healing and marvels, Riots in Temples and marvels, Disturbances at Funerals and marvels, Contempt of Court and marvels, Damage to Property and marvels, Interference with Justice and marvels; and always women and love, women and death, and always the difference between the 'Haves' and the 'Have-nots'!

With women and the opening of the womb this artful doctor begins his story; and with women and the opening of the tomb he ends it;.

And it is certainly not only scientists who have cause to be disturbed by this healing of the sick, this curing the lame, the blind, the deaf, the dumb, without recourse to vivisection. The consistent moralist has every reason to be offended. 'He that is not with me is against me.' 'He that is not against me is with me.' What are we to make of such contradictions? And the unhappy fig-tree? And the drowned swine? And the unfair treatment of the hard-working elder son who got no 'fatted-calf', and the laborious workers who had 'borne the burden and heat of the day' compared with the lucky rogues who slipped in at the eleventh hour? And the subtle, complicated, mysterious ironies, as puzzling to us as to the simple disciples, without making friends with Mammon, and agreeing with Adversary quickly, and paying tribute to Caesar, and letting dead bury their dead? Well, there it is! Had these Gospel-writers been the tricky priests our rationalists call them, would they not have smoothed out these enigmatical creases in the Coat without a Seam?

JOHN COWPER POWYS
The Pleasures of Literature

My Stories are Better

The business in the stable isn't convincing; whereas my atmosphere (vide reviews) can be positively breathed.

JOSEPH CONRAD
Letters of Joseph Conrad

Probably an Illiterate

Had it been the object or the intention of Jesus Christ to establish a new religion, he would undoubtedly have written the system himself, or *procured it to be written* in his lifetime. But there is no publication extant authenticated with his name. All the books called the New Testament were written after his death. He was a Jew by birth and by profession; and he was the Son of God in like manner that every other person is – for the Creator is the father of all.

The first four books, called Matthew, Mark, Luke and John do not give a history of the life of Jesus Christ, but only detached anecdotes of him. It appears from those books, that the whole time of his being a preacher was not more than eighteen months; and it was only during this short time that those men became acquainted with him. They make mention of him at the age of twelve years, sitting, they say, among the Jewish doctors, asking and answering them questions. As this was several years before their acquaintance with him began, it is most probably they had this anecdote from his parents. From this time there is no account of him for about sixteen years. Where he lived, or how he employed himself, during this interval is not known. Most probably he was working at his father's trade, which was that of a carpenter. It does not appear that he had any school education, and the probability is, that he could not write, for his parents were extremely poor, as appears from their not being able to pay for a bed when he was born.

TOM PAINE
The Age of Reason

≕

Take it or Leave it

I cannot, and I will not, separate scripture into *false* and *true*. It is, and it must be, all of a piece. If the miracles took place, so did the incarnation. We are told of both in the same book, and we have no other authority for either.

WILLIAM COBBETT
quoted in George Spater, *William Cobbett*

≕

RESURRECTION

A Most Beautiful Passage

I have been thinking of that most beautiful passage in Luke's Gospel – the appearance of Jesus to the disciples at Emmaus. How universal in its significance! The soul that has hopelessly followed its Jesus – its impersonation of the highest and best – all in despondency; its thoughts all refuted, its dreams all dissipated! Then comes another Jesus – another, but the same – the same highest and best, only chastened – crucified instead of triumphant – and the soul learns that this is the true way to conquest and glory. And then there is the burning of the heart, which assures that 'this was the Lord!' – that this is the inspiration from above – the true comforter that leads unto truth. But I am not become a Methodist, dear Sara; on the contrary, if I am pious one day, you may be sure I was very wicked the day before, and shall be so again the next.

GEORGE ELIOT

J. W. Cross, *Life of George Eliot*

It's Like Reportage

I am to a certain extent an agnostic Catholic. I am quite unable to believe in Hell which contradicts my faith that if there is a God he must be a loving God or else why bother to invent the Devil? As a separate Person? Nor do I accept Rome's teaching on contraception which in this poor overcrowded world goes against all reason – a teaching which in Catholic countries or rather among Catholics is one of the principle reasons of abortion.

One must distinguish between faith and belief. I have faith, but less and less belief, in the existence of God. I have a continuing faith that I am wrong not to believe and that my lack of belief stems from my own faults and failure in love.

Now paradoxically in the affair of Father Hans Kung and Father Schillebeeckx I find myself grateful to those two priests for reawakening my belief – my belief in the empty tomb and the resurrection, the magic side of the Christian religion if you like. Perhaps that is the unconscious mission of Father S. when he writes of the resurrection as being a kind of symbolic statement of the spiritual impression which the apostles experienced after the crucifixion. I remember again in St John's Gospel the run between Peter and John towards the tomb. Peter leading until he lost breath, and then the younger man arriving first and seeing the linen cloths but afraid to go in, and then Peter overtaking him . . . it's like *reportage*. I can be interested in the *reportage* of a mystery: I am completely uninterested – even bored – by a spiritual symbol equally 'unhistoric' in Kung's sense as the *reportage*. The attempt to get rid of the fairy tale makes me for the first time in years begin to believe in it again. I am against the condemnation of Father S. for he has communicated belief to at least one Catholic.

GRAHAM GREENE

L. Duran, *Graham Greene: Friend and Brother*

Fishy

He visited Poros with Patrick Leigh Fermor and Alan Moore-head and read the Gospels for the first time in years. St John's Gospel was, he decided, 'an absolutely staggering document. It has really shaken my paganism, for I think there is much in it that could only be spoken by a god ... On the other hand, I dislike everything else as much as ever e.g. God, Trinity, Virgin M etc.' – and the Resurrection 'seems terribly fishy'.

Connolly put his new-found knowledge of the Bible to good use in the autumn. 'Last night', Barbara recorded, 'Cyril read out the woman taken in adultery – "He that is without sin among you, let him first cast a stone at her." What a beautiful story.'

JEREMY LEWIS

from J. Lewis, *Cyril Connolly: A Life*

A Virtuous and Amiable Man

Nothing that is here said can apply, even with the most distant disrespect to the *real* character of Jesus Christ.

He was a virtuous and amiable man. The morality that he preached and practised was of the most benevolent kind; and though similar systems of morality had been preached by Confucius, and by some of the Greek philosophers, many years before; by the Quakers since; and by many good men in all ages, it has not been exceeded by any.

Jesus Christ wrote no account of himself; of his birth, parentage, or anything else; not a line of what is called the New Testament is of his own writing. The history of him is altogether the work of other people; and as to the account given at his resurrection and ascension, it was the necessary counterpart to the story of his birth. His historians having brought him into the world in a supernatural manner, were obliged to take him out again in the same manner, or the first part of the story must have fallen to the ground.

The wretched contrivance with which this latter part is told, exceeds everything that went before it. The first part, that of the miraculous conception, was not a thing that admitted of publicity, and therefore the tellers of this part of the story had this advantage, that though they might be detected, they could not be expected to prove it, because it was not one of those things that admitted of proof, and it was impossible that the person of whom it was told could prove it himself.

But the resurrection of a dead person from the grave, and his ascension through the air, is a thing very different as to the evidence it admits of, to the invisible conception of a child in the womb. The resurrection and ascension, supposing them to have taken place, admitted of public and ocular demonstration, like that of the ascension of a balloon, or the sun at noon-day, to all Jerusalem at least. A thing which everybody is required to believe, requires that the proof and evidence of it should be equal to all, and universal; and as the public visibility of this last related act was the only evidence that could give sanction to the former part, the whole of it falls to the ground, because that evidence was never given. Instead of this, a small number of persons, not more than eight or nine, are introduced as proxies for the whole world, to say they saw it, and all the rest of the world are called upon to believe it. But it appears that Thomas did not believe the resurrection, and, as they say, would not believe without having ocular and manual demonstration himself. *So neither will I*, and the reason is equally good for me, and for every other person, as for Thomas.

It is in vain to attempt to palliate or disguise this matter. The story, so far as relates to the supernatural part, has every mark of fraud and imposition stamped upon the face of it. Who were the authors of it is as impossible for us now to know, as it is for us to be assured that the books in which the account is related, were written by the persons whose names they bear; the best surviving evidence we now have respecting from the affair is the Jews. They are regularly descended from the people who live in the time this resurrection and ascension is said to have happened, and they say *it is not true*. It has long appeared to me a strange inconsistency to cite the Jews, as a proof of the truth of the story. It is just the same as if a man were to say, I will prove the truth of what I have told you by producing the people who say it is false.

That such a person as Jesus Christ existed, and that he was crucified, which was the mode of execution at that day, are historical relations strictly within the limits of probability. He preached most excellent morality and the equality of man; but he preached also against the corruptions and avarice of the Jewish priests, and this brought upon him the hatred and vengeance of the whole order of priesthood. The accusation which those priests brought against him, was that of sedition and conspiracy against the Roman government, to which the Jews were then subject and tributary; and it is not improbable that the Roman government might have some secret apprehension of the effects of his doctrine as well as the Jewish priests; neither is it improbable that Jesus Christ had in contemplation the delivery of the Jewish nation from the bondage of the Romans. Between the two, however, the virtuous Reformer and Revolutionist lost his life.

It is upon this plain narrative of facts, together with another case I am going to mention, that the Christian mythologists, calling themselves the Christian Church, have erected their fable, which for absurdity and extravagance is not exceeded by anything that is to be found in the mythology of the ancients.

TOM PAINE
The Age of Reason

—⇀

Shivering and Amazed

I suppose there is no event in the whole life of Christ to which, in hours of doubt or fear, men turn with more anxious facts to know the close facts of it, or with earnest and passionate dwelling upon every syllable of its recorded narrative, than Christ's showing Himself to his disciples at the Lake of Galilee. There is something pre-eminently open, natural, full fronting your disbelief, in this manifestation. The others, recorded after the Resurrection, were sudden, phantom-like, occurring to men in profound sorrow and wearied agitation of the heart; not, it might seem, safe judges of what they saw. But the agitation was now over. They had gone back to their daily work, thinking still their business lay net-wards, unmeshed from the literal rope and drag. 'Simon Peter saith unto them, I go a-fishing. They say unto him, We also go with thee.' True words, enough, and having far echo beyond those Galilean hills. That night they caught nothing; but when the morning came, in the clear light of it, behold! a figure stood on the shore. They were not thinking of anything but their fruitless hauls. They had no guess who it was. It asked them simply if they had caught anything. They say, No: and it tells them to cast again. And John shades his eyes from the morning sun with his hands to look who it is; he makes out who it is at last; and poor Simon, not to be outrun this time, tightens his fisher's coat about him, and dashes in over the nets. One would have liked to see him swim those hundred yards and stagger to his knees upon the beach.

Well, the others get to the beach, too, in time, in such slow way as men in general do get to its true shore, much impeded by that wonderful 'dragging the net with fishes'; but they get there – seven of them in all, first the Denier, and then the slowest believer, and then the quickest believer and then the two throne-seekers, and two more, we know not who.

They sit down on the shore, face to face with Him, and eat their broiled fish as He bids. And then to Peter, all dripping still, shivering and amazed, staring at Christ in the sun, on the other side of the coal-fire – thinking a little perhaps of what happened by another coal-fire, when it was colder, and having had no word changed with him by his Master since that look of His – to him so amazed, comes the question, 'Simon, lovest thou me?' Try to feel that a little; and think of it till it is true to you.

JOHN RUSKIN
Modern Painters

Nothing Else Like It in History

The influence of the Resurrection upon the early spread of Jesus' teachings must have been very great. The time thirsted for wonders quite as much as it thirsted for light and leading. At every street corner from Gaul to Babylon stood an itinerant evangelist, preaching some new and bizarre faith, and almost all of them mingled familiar marvels with their novel schemes of salvation. They cured the sick just as Jesus did: they walked on water without sinking and through fire without burning; some of them even professed to raise the dead. But one wonder, at least, they could not perform, and that was precisely the one that people most waited to see: put to death, they could not raise themselves. Nevertheless, no one seems to have thought that it was intrinsically impossible; people stood ready to believe it without too much urging; more, they were willing to accept it as proof positive of the risen prophet's doctrine, for such was the simple logic of the time. Thus we behold even so enlightened a man as Herod made uneasy by the sudden suspicion that Jesus might be the headless John come back again, and thus we hear the chief priests and Pharisees demand of Pilate that he put a guard at Jesus's sepulchre, 'lest his disciples come by night and steal him away, and say unto the people, He is risen from the dead.' The Pharisees, it is plain, had heard that Jesus had been prophesying His own return – if not as the actual Messiah, then at least as one of the fore-runners of the Messiah – and they knew that many poor folk looked for that marvel more or less hopefully and confidently.

The Disciples, it appears, were not among them; they retained their doubts to the last. Instead of following the body of their lost Leader to the sepulchre they left that office to Joseph of Arimathea, a stranger, and to Mary Magdalen, 'the other Mary,' and a small band of lesser pious women. Even when, the next day, the news was brought to them that He had actually arisen from the dead they were still disinclined to believe it, and Luke tells us that Jesus had to convince them by tracking them down and confronting them, and that He upbraided them bitterly for 'their unbelief and hardness of heart.' What actually happened? Unless the whole New Testament is to be rejected as moonshine it seems to be certain that many persons saw Him after His supposed death on the cross, including not a few who were violently disinclined to believe in His Resurrection. Matthew tells us, indeed, that even His arch enemies, the chief priests, were forced to admit the fact of His appearance, and that they sought to account for it, going back to their warning to Pilate, by saying that 'his disciples came by night, and stole him away.' It seems to be equally certain than many persons spoke to Him and heard Him speak, and that He assured them once more that the end of things was at hand.

But what actually happened – on the cross and in the sepulchre? The question has been threshed out between the faithful and the skeptical for many a year, without bringing any answer satisfactory to all parties, or any hope of one hereafter. Fortunately enough, we need not wrestle with it here. The important thing, and the undisputed thing, is that when Jesus was taken from the cross and put into the sepulchre the crowd that looked on, including both His own followers and the Roman soldiers, believed He was truly dead, and that He Himself, when He came to His senses in the sepulchre, believed He was coming back from death. Upon that theory, though it wars upon every rationality that enlightened men cherish, the most civilized section of the human race has erected a structure of ideas and practices so vast in scope and so powerful in effect that the whole range of history showeth nothing parallel.

H.L. MENCKEN
Treatise on the Gods

＝

God Knows!

Resurrection. In form so contrary to all expectation – i.e. no glorification but re-emphasising the shaming wounds of crucifixion. On all the evidence seems very likely indeed. *But not foreseen by the living Jesus.* Last words surely as in *Matthew* and *Mark* – 'My God, My God . . .' Died close to despair. Learned of his special role (beyond mere Messiah) between Friday evening and Sunday morning.

But after the last resurrection appearance – WHAT?

God knows! (And *we* do not. *None* of us does.)

Was he, perhaps taken up into God, in such a way that God himself was changed by this conjunction? Was the all-loving aspect of God enormously strengthened by its work in the life and resurrection and absorption of Jesus Christ?

PHILIP TOYNBEE
End of a Journey

WAS HE GOD?

Dear Friend and Brother

But the wonderful thing is that by devious paths we have got back to Christianity once more, and that the Christ figure appears – to me, at least – more beautiful and understandable than ever. The worst that any sect can do for Christ is to make him incredible. Now he appeared as a great heaven-sent Teacher living a life which was to be our example. That was surely enough without any question of a mystical atonement.

It is not for our mosquito brains to say what degree of divinity was in Him, but we can surely say that He was nearer the divine than we, and that His teaching is the most beautiful of which we have cognisance. So in a circle we have come back to Him – the great, kindly, brooding Spirit who yearns over the world which is His special care. He has ceased to be a miracle. He has become our dear friend and brother.

SIR ARTHUR CONAN DOYLE

My Religion

He Never Defined Sin

This is what I mean by morality versus immorality. Be moral and you get yourself crucified; be immoral and you ruin yourself. 'There was only one Christian and He died on the cross.' There is more truth in this one saying of Nietzsche's than is generally suspected. Jesus did not die on the cross in order that we might have life everlasting. He did not need to die on the cross; he might have given battle to the world and triumphed over it. He might have become the Emperor of the World instead of its scapegoat. He said: 'I have *overcome* the world!' That was a far greater triumph. He overcame the world so thoroughly that it has never been able to get rid of him. 'I am the light of the world,' he proclaimed, and that light still shines. 'The Kingdom of Heaven is within you,' he announced, restoring to every man his divinity and supremacy. When he healed a man or woman, when he cast out the devil, he would say: 'Go and sin no more!' He never defined sin, he never fought against it. He annihilated it by not recognizing it. That is morality and immorality.

HENRY MILLER
Stand Still Like a Hummingbird

Rationalism

I maintain therefore that a man reading the New Testament frankly and freshly would *not* get the impression of what is now often meant by a human selection, like the merely evolutionary man. Moreover there have been too many of these human Christs found in the same story, just as there have been too many keys to mythology found in the same stories. Three or four separate schools of rationalism have worked over the ground and produced three or four equally rational explanations of his life. The first rational explanation of his life is that he never lived. And this in turn gave an opportunity for three or four different explanations; as that he was a sun-myth or a corn-myth, or any other kind of myth that is also a monomania. Then, the idea that he was a divine being who did exist. In my youth it was the fashion to say that he was merely an ethical teacher in the manner of the Essenes, who had apparently nothing very much to say that Hillel or a hundred other Jews might not have said; as that it is a kindly thing to be kind and an assistance to purification to be pure. Then somebody said he was a madman with a Messianic delusion. Then others said he was indeed an original teacher because he cared about nothing but Socialism; or (as others said) about nothing but Pacifism. Then a more grimly scientific character appeared who said that Jesus would never have been heard of at all except for his prophecies of the end of the world. He was important merely as a Millenarian like Dr Cumming; and created a provincial scare by announcing the exact date of the crack of doom. Among other variants on the same theme was the theory that he was a spiritual healer and nothing else; a view implied by Christian Science, which has really to expound a Christianity without the Crucifixion in order to explain the curing of Peter's wife's mother or the daughter of a centurion. There is another theory that concentrates entirely on the business of diabolism and what it would call the contemporary superstition about demoniacs; as if Christ, like a young deacon taking his first orders, had got as far as exorcism and never got any further. Now each of these explanations in itself seems to me singularly inadequate; but taken together they do suggest something of the very mystery which they miss. There must surely have been something not only mysterious but many-sided about Christ if so many smaller Christs can be carved out of him. If the Christian Scientist is satisfied with him as a spiritual healer and the Christian Socialist is satisfied with him as a social reformer, so satisfied that they do not even expect him to be anything else, it looks as if he really covered rather more ground than they could be expected to expect. And it does seem to suggest that there might be more than they fancy in these other mysterious attributes of casting out devils or prophesying doom.

Above all, would not such a new reader of the New Testament stumble over something that would startle him much more than it startles us? I have here more than once attempted the rather impossible task of reversing time and the historic method; and in fancy looking forward to the facts, instead of backward through the memories. So I have imagined the monster that man might have seemed at first to the mere nature around him. We should have a worse shock if we really imagined the nature of Christ named for the first time. What should we feel at the first whisper of a certain suggestion about a certain man? Certainly it is not for us to blame anybody who should find that first wild whisper merely impious and insane. On the contrary, stumbling on that rock of scandal is the first step. Stark staring incredulity is a far more loyal tribute to that truth than a modernist metaphysic that would make it out merely a matter of degree. It were better to rend our robes with a great cry against blasphemy, like Caiaphus in the judgment, or to lay hold of the man as a maniac possessed of devils like the kinsmen and the crowd, rather than to stand stupidly debating fine shades of pantheism in the presence of so catastrophic a claim. There is more of the wisdom that is one with surprise in any simple person, full of the sensitiveness of simplicity, who should expect the grass to wither and the birds to drop dead out of the air, when a strolling carpenter's apprentice said calmly and almost carelessly, like one looking over his shoulder: 'Before Abraham was, I am.'

G.K. CHESTERTON
The Essential G.K. Chesterton

A Terrible Moral Huntsman

It was not merely a moral and a social revolution that Jesus proclaimed; it is clear from a score of indications that his teaching had a political bent of the plainest sort. It is true that he said his kingdom was not of this world, that it was in the hearts of men and not upon the throne; but it is equally clear that wherever and in what measure his kingdom was set up in the hearts of men, the outer world would be in that measure revolutionized and made new.

Whatever else the deafness and blindness of his hearers may have missed in his utterances, it is plain that they did not miss his resolve to revolutionize the world . . .

The whole tenor of the opposition to him and the circumstances of his trial show clearly that to his contemporaries he seemed to propose plainly, and did propose plainly to change and fuse and enlarge all human life. But even his disciples did not grasp the profound and comprehensive significance of that proposal. They were ridden by the old Jewish dream of a king, a Messiah to overthrow the Hellenized Herods and the Roman overlord, and to restore the fabled glories of David. They disregarded the substance of his teaching, plain and direct though it was; evidently they thought it was merely his mysterious and singular way of setting about the adventure that would put him on the throne of Jerusalem. They thought he was just another king among the endless succession of kings, but of a quasi-magic kind and making quasi-magic professions of an impossible virtue.

They thought his life was a stratagem and his death a trick.

He was too great for his disciples. And in view of what he plainly said, is it any wonder that all who were rich and prosperous felt a horror of strange things, a swimming of their world at his teaching? Perhaps the priests and the rulers and the rich men understood him better than his followers. He was dragging out all the little private reservations they had made from social service into the light of a universal religious life. He was like some terrible moral huntsman digging mankind out of the snug burrows in which they had lived hitherto. In the white blaze of this kingdom of his there was to be no property, no privilege, no pride and precedence; no motive indeed and no reward but love. Is it any wonder that men were dazzled and blinded and cried out against him? Even his disciples cried out when he would not spare them the light. Is it any wonder that the priests realized that between this man and themselves there was no choice but that he or priestcraft should perish? Is it any wonder that the Roman soldiers, confronted and amazed by something soaring over their comprehension and threatening all their disciplines, should take refuge in wild laughter, and crown him with thorns and robe him in purple and make a mock Caesar of Him? For to take him seriously was to enter upon a strange and alarming life, to abandon habits, to control instincts and impulses, to essay an incredible happiness . . .

Is it any wonder that to this day this Galilean is too much for our small hearts?

H.G. WELLS
A Short History of the World

All the World Wants a Hero

There met in Jesus Christ all things that can make man lovely and loveable. In his body he was most beautiful. This is known first by the tradition in the Church that it was so and by holy writers agreeing to suit those words to him: Thou art beautiful in mould above the sons of men: we have even accounts of him written in early times. They tell us that he was moderately tall, well built and slender in frame, his features straight and beautiful, his hair inclining to auburn, parted in the midst, curling and clustering about the ears and neck as the leaves of a filbert, so they speak, upon the nut. He wore also a forked beard and this as well as the locks upon his head were never touched by a razor or shears; neither, his health being perfect, could a hair ever fall to the ground. The account I have been quoting (it is from memory, for I cannot now lay my hand upon it) we do not indeed for certain know to be correct, but it has been current in the Church and many generations have drawn our Lord accordingly either in their own minds or in his images. Another proof of his beauty may be drawn from the words *proficiebat sapientia et aetate et gratia apud Deum et homines* (Luc. ii 52), he went forward in wisdom and bodily frame and favour with God and men; that is, he pleased both God and men daily more and more by his growth of mind and body. But he could not have pleased by growth of body unless the body was strong, healthy, and beautiful that grew. But the best proof of all this, that his body was the special work of the Holy Ghost. He was not born in nature's course, no man was his father; had he been born as others are he must have inherited some defect of figure or of constitution, from which no man born as fallen men are born is wholly free unless God interfere to keep him so. But his body was framed directly from heaven by the power of the Holy Ghost, of whom it would be unworthy to leave any the least botch or failing in his work. So the first Adam was moulded by God himself and Eve built up by God too out of Adam's rib and they could not but be pieces, both, of faultless workmanship: the same then and much more must Christ have been. His constitution too was tempered perfectly, he had neither disease nor the seeds of any: weariness he felt when he was wearied, hunger when he fasted, thirst when he had long gone without drink, but to the touch of sickness he was a stranger. I leave it to you brethren, then to picture him, in whom the fulness of the godhead dwelt bodily, in his bearing how majestic, how strong and yet how lovely and lissome in his limbs, in his look how earnest, grave but kind. In his Passion all this strength was spent, this lissomness crippled, this beauty wrecked, this majesty beaten down. But now it is more than all restored, and for myself I make no secret I look forward with eager desire to seeing the matchless beauty of Christ's body in the heavenly light.

GERARD MANLEY HOPKINS
Gerard Manley Hopkins

No Historical Jesus

You ought not to bother about the Jesus of History. There is no Jesus of History. The only history of Jesus is Mark, & what a wretched skimpy ill told tale it is & how next to impossible to make out anything from it, & how simple a soul he was who wrote it, & how little he could have known Christ. The law court part is fairly full, but it always makes me feel that Mark only knew Christ right at the end of his career. Matthew may have known Mark & had some other material as well, & hated the Jews & gave them some nasty jabs by the way. Luke was an educated man who wanted to make the story palatable to the Romans. I don't think he knew Christ at all, nor Matthew either for that matter. But these are the only authorities we have for the Jesus of History. We know more about Jack Sheppard & Dick Turpin.

The Jesus of Faith is not much more real today. I have seen no modern representation of him which did not make him an anaemic imbecile. I saw the big Italian movey of him. It made him about as live as an elderly sheep that has been eating ivy. I have more sympathy with a good old fire and brimstone Satan any day. But when we come to the Jesus of the Imagination, then we come to a tremendous figure; & by thought & brooding over the poor skimpy ill-told gospels this figure, comes up & is heroic, & you see a swift keen Jew, with the clearest & quickest kind of mind, great courage, great wit, & a kind of extraordinary rightness of conduct such as only comes from clear & swift & big imagination. With this figure in one's heart, the greasy, servile, white lamb & tortured gentleman idea of him becomes most loathsome & awful. Jesus in his wit & in anger would have shrivelled up such a creature with one glance. So burn your new book, my good lady, or better still sell it & buy some nice little blasphemy by Voltaire or Anatole France with the large sums you will surely receive in its stead.

JOHN MASEFIELD
Letters of John Masefield to Florence Lamont

A Great Artist

Our Lord was probably born in Nazareth in Galilee in the summer and not in Bethlehem in Judea in the winter. But what is important is that he was born at all. And those who say he never lived are stealing him from mankind just as surely as they who say he was God.

It is, of course, possible that there is a God, but what is absolutely impossible is that Jesus of Nazareth thought he was God. Not even the craziest Jew in history could believe that, let alone the sanest. In the Hebrew world God was God and that was that. The nearest they got to him was the light around his throne. There is a magnificent Hebrew word for it. Our Lord believed in God, he believed in Him very much, but he also believed in us. To Our Lord the Kingdom of Heaven meant the Commonwealth of Man. He loved life and wanted everyone to live beautifully. And he died willingly that they might learn how.

Being a great artist, and his art was the greatest art in the world, that of living properly, he probably thought that God was getting a bit fed up with all those offerings of animals and birds that were consistently being killed as sacrifices to him. So he offered himself to God, so that God would teach people to make a great poem of their lives on this earth. He who knew how to live better than anyone to whom life had been given, gave up that life, at 31 or 33, so that others might enjoy theirs into their seventies.

He danced at the wedding feast of Cana. He was as Jewish as the Old Testament, as Hebrew as the fields he walked through, as beautiful as the Galilee he loved, and it is beautiful. He loved freedom, hated bullies. Indeed he was a poet. At times he was almost Yiddish.

. . .

Our Lord, Jesus of Nazareth, the child of Joseph the carpenter and Mary his wife, working-class Jewish people and not their only child either (Our Lord had three brothers and two sisters: history knows the names of his brothers, but not of his sisters) was indeed a man among men, sometimes I even think of him as a good man fallen among goys, was perhaps the loveliest human being ever to have lived on this earth. The moral grandeur of his conception of life as told in those great poems, his parables, has never been equalled before or since.

That is why people with no faith in man, try either to say he was God, or that he did not live at all. One can see how it happened, how the Hebrew conception of God, which was the highest conceived by man, was watered down to suit the beautiful Hellenist conception of life. How this Jewish poet, with his tired feet – he walked an awful lot – was turned into a Greek God. But even as a God his Hebrew humanity keeps on coming through. He is better than any other God. But he would have hated what Christianity has become just as much as Marx would have hated Communism in its Soviet form.

During his lifetime and for centuries before, Israel, this little nation that had freed the world from idolatry, was looking for the Messiah. Our Lord being a great spiritual artist – all the Jews had that was first rate was their religion, the Greeks were their superiors in most other things – had a different conception of the function of the Messiah from that of priests and politicians. He thought that the Messiah himself should suffer, not that the people should suffer more as a prelude to his coming. For the most part the world has misunderstood him, for the most part his own disciples misunderstood him. Yet after he died they spent the rest of their lives, and willingly gave up those lives, for their conception of his ideas. They did not forget him. They conquered the world with a story, his story. A few young fishermen from the sea of Galilee started a movement from their rowing boats on an inland lake, now believed in by the Captain of the Queen Mary, crossing the Atlantic, an ocean they did not even know existed. Our Lord indeed may not have risen from the dead, but in those forty-three days between the first Good Friday and the first Pentecost something did happen. On Good Friday, everyone, except the women funked it. From Pentecost onwards they all lived like heroes and died like men.

PAUL POTTS
Dante Called You Beatrice

A Gentle Link

The beautiful figure of Christ appears to me as a necessary device to soften our terror of the unknown creator; a gentle link, a semi-human advocate.

VITA SACKVILLE-WEST
This I Believe

Not Like General Boulanger

If Jesus had been a man [he explained, towards the end of his life], He could not do anything for me. How can people represent Him like that? Like a bigger and better [General] Boulanger? What would that mean to me? If I am to be saved from my misery, I need a God, not a person who once lived on earth, a person whose life can be reconstructed with the help of documents . . . Oh, the fools who think that Jesus is contained within a few wretched little books! Do they believe, then, that Christianity has derived from the Gospels? . . . No, no, it's the poor little working-class women who have faithfully kept the memories of the Passion and the Cross; it is Nero, maker of martyrs, who saved belief in Christ and made it into a thing of grief and blood. For me, Jesus is The Crucified. He is my God because He suffered, because He suffers still. I see Him before my eyes, covered with dreadful wounds, sweating in His final agony, as the peasant women of Judea actually saw Him.

PAUL VERLAINE
quoted in J. Richardson, *Verlaine*

An Extraordinary Being

These are the kind of thoughts which in combination create the impression that Christianity is something weak and diseased. First, for instance, that Jesus was a gentle creature, sheepish and unworldly, a mere ineffectual appeal to the world; second, that Christianity arose and flourished in the dark ages of ignorance, and that to these the Church would drag us back; third, that the people still strongly religious or (if you will) superstitious – such people as the Irish – are weak, unpractical, and behind the times. I only mention these ideas to affirm the same thing; that when I looked into them independently I found, not that the conclusions were unphilosophical, but simply that the facts were not facts. Instead of looking at books and pictures about the New Testament I looked at the New Testament. There I found an account not in the least of a person with his hair parted in the middle or his hands clasped in appeal, but of an extraordinary being with lips of thunder and acts of lurid decision, flinging down tables, casting out devils, passing with the wild secrecy of the wind from mountain isolation to a sort of dreadful demagogy; a being who often acted like an angry god – and always like a god. Christ has even a literary style of his own, not to be found, I think elsewhere; it consists of an almost furious use of the *a fortiori*. His 'how much more' is piled one upon another like castle upon castle in the clouds. The diction used *about* Christ has been, and perhaps wisely, sweet and submissive. But the diction used by Christ is quite curiously gigantesque; it is full of camels leaping through needles and mountains hurled into the sea. Morally it is equally terrific; he called himself a sword of slaughter, and told men to buy swords if they sold their coats for them. That he used other even wilder words on the side of non-resistance greatly increases the mystery; but it also, if anything, rather increases the violence. We cannot even explain it by calling such a being insane; for insanity is usually along one consistent channel. The maniac is generally a monomaniac. Here we must remember the difficult definition of Christianity already given; Christianity is a superhuman paradox whereby two opposite passions may blaze beside each other. The one explanation of the Gospel language that does explain it, is that it is the survey of one who from some supernatural height beholds some more startling synthesis.

G.K. CHESTERTON
Orthodoxy

Scarcely Visible

Jesus of Nazareth: that scarcely visible young man; but from whom light streams forward into the New Testament, into the early Church, into all later history . . .

PHILIP TOYNBEE
End of a Journey

⊷

British Bulldog

Setting aside the huge mass of inculcated Christ-worship which has no real significance because it has no intelligence, there is, among people who are really free to think for themselves on the subject, a great deal of hearty dislike of Jesus and of contempt for his failure to save himself and overcome his enemies by personal bravery and cunning as Mahomet did. I have heard this feeling expressed far more impatiently by persons brought up in England as Christians than by Mahometans, who are, like their prophet, very civil to Jesus, and allow him a place in their esteem and veneration at least as high as we accord to John the Baptist. But this British bulldog contempt is founded on a complete misconception of his reasons for submitting voluntarily to an ordeal of torment and death. The modern Secularist is often so determined to regard Jesus as a man like himself and nothing more, that he slips unconsciously into the error of assuming that Jesus shared that view. But it is quite clear from the New Testament writers (the chief authorities for believing that Jesus ever existed) that Jesus at the time of his death believed himself to be the Christ, a divine personage. It is therefore absurd to criticize his conduct before Pilate as if he were Colonel Roosevelt or Admiral von Tirpitz or even Mahomet. Whether you accept his belief in his divinity as fully as Simon Peter did, or reject it as a delusion which led him to submit to torture and sacrifice his life without resistance in the conviction that he would presently rise again in glory, you are equally bound to admit that, far from behaving like a coward or a sheep, he shewed considerable physical fortitude in going through a cruel ordeal against which he could have defended himself as effectually as he cleared the money-changers out of the temple. 'Gentle Jesus, meek and mild' is a snivelling modern invention, with no warrant in the gospels. St Matthew would as soon have thought of applying such adjectives to Judas Maccabeus as to Jesus; and even St Luke, who makes Jesus polite and gracious, does not make him meek. The picture of him as an English curate of the farcical comedy type, too meek to fight a policeman, and everybody's butt, may be useful in the nursery to soften children; but that such a figure could ever have become a centre of the world's attention is too absurd for discussion: grown men and women may speak kindly of a harmless creature who utters amiable sentiments and is a helpless nincompoop when he is called on to defend them; but they will not follow him, nor do what he tells them, because they do not wish to share his defeat and disgrace.

BERNARD SHAW
Preface to *Androcles and the Lion*

Cruel, Ambiguous Words

So then we come back to this. If Christ's loving words are to ring out strongly, and his cruel and ambiguous words to cast no shadow upon them, then (or so it seems to me) we had better say: He was not divine, he was not God incarnate, he was not the Second Person of the Trinity, and there is no Trinity.

Need we love him less? I do not think so, but rather perhaps more. His teaching about the Kingdom, his strange parables, the curious love he had for our not very lovable race, his quick discernment of hypocrisy, his contempt for material values, for these things one must love him. And there are other things too, or rather there is the one overwhelming thing – his teaching about Love. And that God is Love. In the late Roman world of his day, in the seedy cynicism of the Empire's religious upholstery, how this teaching runs and flashes. And if this teaching about love that burns with such seeming freshness does not, in history's facts, turn out to be the first time such things were said, if for instance (and so near the time of Jesus) that great teacher and philosopher, the superb Hillel, first said many of the words that Christ said, even so, the words them-selves are good, and to put those words upon the lips of a god, and to worship that God – such a God as who, in the abjection of a miserable death (miserable, but alas common enough – how many Jews did Titus crucify before the walls of Jerusalem?) could pray for his tormentors: 'Father, forgive them, for they know not what they do' – at least we may say: This was a new sort of God, this was indeed a Step Forward.

I am aware, too, that there are ways of circumventing the wretched doctrine of eternal hell, set out so large in the New Testament. One way is to say that Christ was a poet and used Hell as a figure of the appallingness of becoming entirely sinful. And if the blood-drenched centuries have taken it in another sense, that is their fault. I do not think this is a road the Christian can take. For if hell is but a figure of evil, then by the same reckoning, God may be but a figure of good. Which may be true, but it is not a Christian truth; it is an argument that offers no objection to atheism, no objection at all. Another point that will be brought forwards, is: that if Christ was no more than a prophet and a poet, how did the Church take root at all, let alone grow strong and survive the centuries? I do not know. Any more than I know why Mohammed – from *very* unlikely beginnings – should have founded and given his name to another great religion. Any more than I know why, in equally unlikely circumstances, a handful of revolutionaries, with the highest aspirations for the good of mankind, should have delivered so large a portion of the human race to the glum government of modern communism.

STEVIE SMITH
Me Again

Heroical Virtues

What touching grace in His instructions! What sweetness, yet what purity, in His manners! What loftiness in His maxims! What profound wisdom in His disclosures! What presence of mind, what delicacy of art, yet what justice, in His replies! What an empire of His passions! Where is the man, where the sage, who knows thus to act, to suffer, and to die, without weakness, and without ostentation? What prejudice, what blindness, must be in him who dares to compare the son of Sophroniscus with the Son of Mary? What a distance lies between them! Greece abounded in virtuous men before he (Socrates) had defined virtue. But when had Jesus drawn for His disciples that exalted and pure morality of which He alone has presented at once the lessons and the example? Out of the midst of the fiercest fanaticism the highest wisdom made itself heard, and the artlessness of the most heroical virtues glorified the vilest of the nations. The death of Socrates, philosophizing quietly with his friends, is the pleasantest that one could desire: that of Jesus, expiring amid torments, insulted, railed at, cursed by a whole nation, is the most horrible that anyone could fear. Socrates, taking the poisoned cup, blesses him who presents it, and who weeps beside him. Jesus, in the midst of a frightful anguish, prays for his maddened executioners. Yes! If the life and the death of Socrates are those of a philosopher, the life and the death of Jesus are those of a God.

JEAN-JACQUES ROUSSEAU

Emile

✐

He Came to Comfort

Man was in a dark place. Christ came to comfort. Why man had to be in a dark place we do not and cannot know, for our half-grown brains obviously cannot grasp the whole truth about the universe.

REBECCA WEST

My Religion

✐

WHO'S WHO

Matthew Arnold 1822–88
Poet and critic, Arnold was educated at Oxford where he became a fellow of Oriel College before the age of thirty and later Professor of Poetry. His verse was first published in 1849, but the bulk of his prose work, attacking what he saw as the prevailing philistinism in England, didn't appear until the 1860s. This critical work was driven partly by his parallel career as an inspector of schools where he struggled to improve secondary education.

In 1851 he married Frances Wightman and three sons were born, all of whom died within a short space of each other; two daughters survived. In later life he applied himself almost exclusively to works of religious criticism, the best known being *Literature and Dogma*.

W.H. Auden 1907–73
Poet and essayist born in York, Auden studied at Oxford in the 1930s where he developed his passion for poetry (his own and others') among an illustrious circle that included John Betjeman and Louis MacNeice. In 1936 he travelled to Spain as a civilian in support of the Republicans, reporting on the conflict with Christopher Isherwood with whom he also collaborated on three verse dramas.

He emigrated to the US in 1939, taking citizenship in 1946. It was here that he converted to Anglicanism and began his peripatetic routine of spending the winters in America and the summers in Europe. Between 1956 and 1961 he was Oxford's elected Professor of Poetry, coming home for good in 1972. He died in Vienna in 1973. Auden's star briefly shone again in the early 1990s when his poem 'Funeral Blues' featured in the hit British film, *Four Weddings and a Funeral*.

A.J. Ayer 1910–89

One of Britain's most distinguished twentieth-century philosophers, Ayer was born in London and educated at Eton and later Oxford, where he was a pupil of Gilbert Ryle. He was later professor at University College, London, and then at Oxford between 1947 and 1959. But it was his acquaintanceship with the Vienna circle of philosphers during the 1930s that was to form the basis of Ayer's most important work and whose anti-metaphysical doctrines he detailed in his first and best book, *Language, Truth and Logic* in 1936.

Ayer's ideas scandalised established philosophy and made him the talk of young dons who would gather in Isaiah Berlin's rooms at All Souls College, Oxford. Ayer, a lifelong atheist, was married four times, twice to the same American woman, Alberta Chapman. His various marriages produced two sons and a daughter and he had a second daughter with the Hollywood columnist Sheilah Graham. Ayer's later works included *The Problem of Knowledge* in 1956 and *The Central Questions of Philosophy* in 1972. He was knighted in 1970.

Arnold Bennett 1867–1931

Industrious novelist, critic and man of letters, Bennett was born in Staffordshire to a bookish, music-loving Methodist family. He studied at London University for a law degree that he never took and worked afterwards as a solicitor's clerk before turning to journalism. He published his first novel *The Man from the North* in 1898 and claimed it to be 'unlike all English novels except those of one author' (George Moore). In 1907 he married a Frenchwoman in Paris where he remained writing until his return to England in 1912.

The *Dictionary of National Biography* describes Bennett as 'perhaps doing too many things not quite well enough to consolidate a single reputation'. But the publication in 1910 of the first volume of his *Clayhanger* trilogy secured his reputation as a serious novelist. Bennett was also an influential reviewer in the *New Age* and his journals were published posthumously.

William Blake 1757–1827

Poet, painter, engraver and rebellious mystic, Blake was born in London and developed one of his talents as an apprentice engraver to the Society of Antiquaries. Blake's unique illustrations were printed with copper plates and then coloured either by himself or his wife, market gardener's daughter Catherine Boucher from Battersea, described as 'one of the best wives that ever fell to the lot of a man of genius'.

Blake's life was one of profound and prolific achievement, abetted by an ardent belief in freedom of the imagination and the power of the spirit of love. This passion united with his unusual creativity to produce a huge body of work including *Songs of Innocence and of Experience*, *The Marriage of Heaven and Hell* and his poem 'Jerusalem', which was later set to music by Sir Hubert Parry and became the great standard bearer for the English hymn.

Thomas Carlyle 1795–1881

Scottish-born essayist and historian, Carlyle studied Divinity at Edinburgh University. Wider reading led to the abandonment of his orthodox views and with them his ambitions for the Ministry. For several years Carlyle worked as a schoolmaster, struggling to find direction and stay afloat financially, a period which fostered his sympathy for the misery of the lower classes. It was during this time that Carlyle began to suffer from the dyspepsia that was to dog for him for the rest of his days and may explain the irritability and gloom in his work.

By the turn of the century he was writing regularly and absorbed in German literature, notably Goethe. In 1826 he married diarist Jane Baillie Welsh who supported him through his frequent depressions and ill health. Carlyle moved to London in the 1830s where he wrote major works on the French Revolution and Frederick the Great. After the death of his wife he retired from public life and wrote little.

G.K. Chesterton 1874–1936

Journalist, novelist, poet and critic, Chesterton was born in London and studied at the Slade School of Art before turning to writing. His work was brought to a wide audience through his *Father Brown* series of books about an amiable detective-priest, but at the height of his popularity he would claim no other title than that of journalist, delighting in his carelessness with facts and references. His best-known work, *Orthodoxy*, was published in 1908 and described by the author as a 'sort of slovenly autobiography ... my ultimate attitude toward life.'

The industrious Chesterton produced an astonishing volume of work, the best of which appeared in the form of social and literary criticism for periodicals, including his own, *G.K.'s Weekly*. His social and religious beliefs were profoundly influenced by two separate but simultaneous unions: his friendship with Hilaire Belloc and his engagement to Anglo-Catholic Frances Blogg around the turn of the century. He converted to Catholicism in 1922, an event which was to inform all of his subsequent writing including *The Everlasting Man* and *St Francis of Assisi*, though he was acclaimed, too, for his critical studies of Dickens, Stevenson and Browning.

William Cobbett 1763–1835

Journalist and reformer, Cobbett was a remarkable character born in Surrey, of peasant origin, and entirely self-educated. Moving on impulse to London at the age of twenty-one, Cobbett spent a year reading widely then signed up to the army, serving in New Brunswick. In 1792 he settled in Philadelphia, lampooning democratic government under the name 'Peter Porcupine'. He returned to Britain in 1800 to start his famous *Political Register* whose Tory sympathies lasted only two years before he changed it overnight into a journal of uncompromising radicalism.

Much of Cobbett's life was spent dodging and defending libel actions as a result of his outspoken criticism and for many years he bounced between England and the US, fleeing legal action and/or imprisonment from both sides. In 1810 he was imprisoned for two years for criticising military flogging. During the 1820s, Cobbett was able to indulge his passion for the land and defence of the rural poor when he undertook a series of political tours, travelling England on horseback. His accounts of the journeys were published in collected form to become his most famous work, *Rural Rides*. He became MP for Oldham in 1832, three years before his death.

John Stewart Collis 1900–84

A remarkable writer about nature in the tradition of W.H. Hudson, Collis was born in Dublin to a bourgeois Anglo-Irish family, raised in County Wicklow and educated at Rugby and

Oxford. During the Second World War he became a farm labourer – an experience that inspired his book, *The Worm Forgives the Plough*, now widely regarded as a classic. He wrote a number of books about scientific phenomena but only achieved recognition with the publication of his memoirs, *Bound Upon a Course*.

A formidably unusual man, Collis endured a lifetime of misfortune and neglect, unloved by his mother and later his first wife. It was only in his last ten years that a second marriage ushered in a period of great happiness and fulfilment. Towards the end of his life he was a regular contributor to the *Spectator*. A.N. Wilson described him as looking 'as if he's been in an open boat for ninety years'.

Cyril Connolly 1903–74

The doyen of literary critics, Connolly was educated at Eton, a contemporary of George Orwell and Anthony Powell. From 1939 to 1950 he edited the influential literary magazine *Horizon*. His best-known book, *Enemies of Promise* (1938), is part autobiography, part reflection on the writer's life. An inveterate hedonist, Connolly was married three times.

Joseph Conrad 1857–1924

Master mariner and successful novelist of brooding and melancholy temperament, Conrad has always appealed to makers of film and television. Born in the Ukraine to Polish parents, he joined the British merchant navy and became a British national in 1886. *Almayer's Folly*, his first novel, was published in 1895 and was swiftly followed by others, including *The Nigger of the Narcissus*, *Lord Jim*, *Nostromo* and *Heart of Darkness*, his prophetic short novel on twentieth-century themes.

In 1895 he married bookseller's daughter Jessie George and settled in Ashford, Kent, where they had two sons. Conrad endured long periods of illness, money worries and discouragement of every sort, working doggedly on until the great moment in 1914 when his novel *Chance* was published in New York. The sensational achievement of having created such fine prose from a language not his own, made him one of the most discussed and praised writers of the age.

E. E. Cummings 1894–1962

Painter and poet, Cummings was born in Cambridge, MA, and studied at Harvard before serving in France in the First World War and spending three months in an internment camp, an experience described in his best-known prose work, *The Enormous Room* (1922). Afterwards he stayed in Paris to study fine art.

During the 1920s Cummings developed rapidly as a poet, becoming famous for his unorthodox typography and linguistic style, but it was a mystical reverence for the wholeness and immediacy of life which drove his work. His first collection *Tulips and Chimneys* was published in 1923, though his *Complete Poems* did not appear until 1960. Twice married, Cummings had one daughter.

Sir Arthur Conan Doyle 1859–1930

Writer and creator of Sherlock Holmes, Conan Doyle was born in Edinburgh and worked as a medical practitioner until poverty made him turn to writing. He introduced his famous supersleuth and the detection mythology associated with Baker Street in his first book, *A Study in Scarlet*, in 1887. His short stories, *The Adventures of Sherlock Holmes*, were serialized in *Strand Magazine* and hailed as masterpieces of detective fiction. But Conan Doyle set greater store by his historical romances, such as *The White Company* (1891), and at one point he became so tired of his popular creation that he killed him off. Holmes had to stage a dramatic recovery when Conan Doyle was compelled to revive him in 1902.

In between times, he served as a physician in the Boer War and was awarded a knighthood for his writing on the South African conflict. Twice married, Conan Doyle converted from Catholicism to Spiritualism in later life and wrote widely on the subject.

George Eliot 1819–80

Born Mary Ann Evans in Warwickshire, Eliot had an evangelical education and wrote scores of devotional poems before renouncing the church's doctrines in her twenties. An accomplished woman, Eliot began her career translating Strauss's *The Life of Jesus* from German and writing critical examinations of society and literature.

Eliot and her beloved George Lewes defied Victorian mores by living in sin for twenty-four years. Though Eliot will be remembered for *Middlemarch* and *The Mill on the Floss*, she was also the author of racy titles such as, *Lust and Inconstancy of Woman: Written by a Lady in Vindication of her Sex.*

Alice Thomas Ellis b. 1932

Born in Liverpool, Alice Thomas Ellis is one of the country's most highly regarded novelists. The mother of seven, she was educated at Bangor Grammar School and Liverpool School of Art; she first took up writing after the death of one of her sons, publishing her first novel, *The Sin Eater*, in 1977. She has gone on to write many widely praised novels, including *Unexplained Laughter*, *The Skeleton in the Cupboard*, *The Clothes in the Wardrobe* and *The Inn at the Edge of the World*, which was adapted for film.

In 1956 she married publisher, Colin Haycraft and in between raising her children was fiction editor for Duckworth, discovering Beryl Bainbridge and Caroline Blackwood among others. During the 1980s she wrote the 'Home Life' column in the *Spectator* and began to devote her energies to exposing 'madness' in the Catholic Church. The scourge of progressives everywhere, Ellis was sacked from the *Catholic Herald* for her views, but continues to agitate through the pages of the *Oldie* where she writes the 'God Slot'.

Havelock Ellis 1859–1939

Physician and writer, Ellis was born in Croydon and travelled extensively in Australia and South America – intrepid for the time – before settling down to study medicine. His explorations on the subject of sex caused something of a stir, he being the first man to put aside Victorian hysteria and treat it with thoroughness and detachment.

Ellis devoted thirty years of his life to the completion of his seven-volume *Studies in the Psychology of Sex*, a labour of love sustained and inspired by personal experience and his devotion to the field of human biology.

Shusaku Endo 1923–96

Widely regarded as Japan's leading writer, Endo was born in Tokyo and studied French literature at Keio University, after which he continued his education in France. His novels include *Silence* (1966), *The Sea and Poison* (1972), *Wonderful Fool* (1974), *Volcano* (1978), *When I Whistle* (1979) and *Stained Glass Elegies* (1984). In 1981 he was elected to the Japanese Arts Academy, the Nihon Geijutsuin. An early convert to Catholicism, Endo wrote his bestselling *Life of Jesus* (1973) to introduce Christ to the non-Christian Japanese.

Mary Gordon 1949–81

A native New Yorker, Mary Gordon was educated at Barnard College where she later taught. She wrote four novels, *The Other Side*, *Final Payments*, *In the Company of Women* and *Men and Angels* as well as a collection of short stories, *Temporary Shelter*. Her work often demonstrated the conflict between her feminist ideals and her commitment to Roman Catholicism.

Robert Graves 1895–1985

High-minded poet and novelist, Graves was born in London, educated at Charterhouse and Oxford, and served in the trenches in the First World War. He was Professor of Literature at Cairo University in the 1920s and at Oxford in the 1960s where he carried out translations of Latin and Greek texts.

In 1918, he married Ben Nicholson's sister, Annie, and together they had two daughters and two sons, but in 1929 he set up house with the American poet Laura Riding. They chose the mountain village of Deja in Majorca where Graves was to live on and off for the rest of his life. Laura left him ten years later for Schuyler Jackson. In 1950 Graves married Beryl Hodge and they had three sons and a daughter. Graves made his name with his novel *I, Claudius* (1934) which was adapted for television in 1976. He also wrote several works of autobiography, notably *Goodbye to All That* and *Occupation Writer* and two well-respected works on Jesus, *The Nazarene Gospel Restored* and *King Jesus*. Graves considered himself first and foremost a poet and when his *Collected Poems* were published in 1975, they drew on more than twenty volumes.

Graham Greene 1904–91

One of the foremost novelists of the twentieth century, Greene was born in Berkhampstead in Hertfordshire and educated at Oxford where he converted to Catholicism. He started out on the staff of *The Times* before turning his hand to fiction. Many of Greene's novels, including *Brighton Rock, The Power and the Glory* and *The Third Man*, have central religious themes, but his early works – *The Man Within* and *Stamboul Train* – are written in a melodramatic, thriller style.

In 1927 he married Vivienne Dayrell-Browning and they had one son and one daughter. They later separated and Greene lived in Antibes in the south of France until his death. Restless and easily bored he travelled widely, taking a special interest in revolutionary politics and the Catholic church.

Thomas Hardy 1840–1928
The darling of Examination Boards up and down the land, Thomas Hardy is widely considered to be a jewel in the crown of English Literature. Born in Dorset to a modest family of passionate music lovers, Hardy studied architecture in Dorchester before leaving for London at the age of twenty-two to write poetry eulogising the rural life he had left behind. Failing to find a publisher, he turned to fiction and found success with *Far From the Madding Crowd* in 1874.

In the same year he married Emma Gifford, a woman who inspired reams of passionate poetry, but it was his novels which have secured his place in the history books. *The Return of the Native, The Mayor of Casterbridge, Jude the Obscure* and *Tess of the d'Urbervilles* have all become classic texts; the latter made into a film by Roman Polanski in 1979.

Heinrich Heine 1797–1856
Dusseldorf-born poet and essayist of Jewish parentage, Heine studied banking and law but by his early twenties had already begun to publish poetry. In 1825 he became a Christian in order to secure German citizenship and in doing so alienated his family and the larger Jewish community. His revolutionary

opinions made him unemployable, but by 1827 his reputation as a poet was established with the publication of his four-volume *Reisebilder* and *Buch der Lieder,*.

After the 1830 revolution Heine went into voluntary exile in Paris and turned his attention away from poetry to politics, becoming leader of the cosmopolitan democratic movement. He spent the rest of his life writing widely on French and German culture.

Gerard Manley Hopkins 1844–89

Priest and poet, Hopkins was born in Essex and educated at Oxford where, under the influence of the Oxford Movement, he became a Catholic. He studied for the priesthood with Jesuits in north Wales and for a while was Professor of Greek at Trinity College, Dublin.

Hopkins wrote poetry throughout his life but never saw a single poem published. They were only brought to public attention through the efforts of his literary executor, Robert Bridges, and in 1930 a collection was published to wide acclaim.

Aldous Huxley 1894–1963

Novelist, essayist and mind-traveller, Huxley was the grandson of T.H. Huxley, from whom he inherited the scientific interest that made him one of the earliest advocates of LSD as a means of achieving 'some over-all understanding of the world'. Born in Surrey, Huxley was educated at Oxford and spent most of the 1920s in Italy where he befriended D.H. Lawrence and wrote many novels including *Point Counter Point* and *Brave New World*, a book which examined the dehumanizing effect of the scientific age.

In 1919 he married Maria Nys whom he had met through Ottoline Morrell at Garsington and they had one son. In 1937 he moved to California in order to immerse himself in mystic searching. It was the perfect location for his later experiments with hallucinogenics, described in his cult text, *The Doors of Perception*, embraced by free-thinkers everywhere. Others were not so impressed and the critic Cyril Connolly said of him, 'Nobody since Chesterton has so squandered his gifts.'

Richard Jefferies 1848–87

Born in Swindon, Jefferies was one of the great Victorian nature writers who, in a life shortened by tuberculosis, wrote some twenty-three books about country life as well as eleven novels. Jefferies wrote passionately about the countryside and its people, agitating on behalf of the poor farm labourer under the excellent appellation, 'Rural Dynamite'.

After an unsuccessful attempt to travel the United States in 1865, Jefferies returned to his birthplace to work freelance on publications such as the *North Wilts Herald* and the *Pall Mall Gazette*. Staunchly opposed to asceticism, he believed that one should aim to enjoy life and his philosophy permeated his writing.

Samuel Johnson 1709–84

The son of a Staffordshire bookseller, Johnson was educated at Lichfield and Oxford and for a short time was a schoolmaster, one of his pupil's being David Garrick. In 1737 he went to London and worked as a journalist in Grub Street before, ten years later, embarking on his famous *Dictionary of the English Language*, a project that took eight years to complete.

A melancholy and profoundly religious man Johnson wrote moralistic essays and biographies of English poets but is best remembered today as the central figure in James Boswell's famous biography which records many examples of his verbal wit and wisdom.

John Keats 1795–1821

Revered poet, John Keats was born in a livery stable in London and studied medicine until he was introduced to Shelley and the other young Romantics, prompting his devotion to verse and the publication of his first sonnets by the age of twenty-one.

In 1820 his landmark collection, *Lamia and Other Poems* was published. Struggling with tuberculosis, he sailed for Italy that year, at the invitation of Shelley, and died in Rome. He is the author of the mythological epic *Endymion* and his *Letters* are among the most celebrated in the English language.

D.H. Lawrence 1885–1930

Novelist, poet and essayist, Lawrence was born in Nottingham where he attended University College before working as a schoolmaster. Ill health and the success of his first novel *The White Peacock* (1911) persuaded him to forsake teaching in order to write. The following year he eloped with his professor's wife, Frieda Weekley, and they lived variously in Germany, Italy and Mexico.

Lawrence's work always created a stir and in 1915 he was prosecuted for obscenity after writing *The Rainbow*. But it was the sensational 1960 obscenity trial over *Lady Chatterley's Lover* that made Lawrence a household name. The novel was not published in unexpurgated form in Britain until thirty-two years after it was written. His other novels include *Women in Love*, made famous by Ken Russell's film.

Norman Mailer b. 1923

The ageing *enfant terrible* of American letters and champion of obscenity, Mailer is his country's foremost contemporary writer. Educated at Harvard and the Sorbonne, he has made a career out of blurring the lines between fiction and reporting. He made his name with his first novel, *The Naked and the Dead*, followed by many others, including *An American Dream, Tough Guys Don't Dance* and *The Deer Park*. His subjects of biography have been diverse, from Marilyn Monroe to the murderer Gary Gilmore, about whom he wrote the excellent *The Executioner's Song*.

Four times married and the father of six children, Mailer is a superb journalist who never shirks a challenge. The scale of his range and ambition was there for all to see in his recent biography of Jesus, *The Gospel According to the Son*.

John Masefield 1878–1967

Herefordshire-born Poet Laureate and novelist, John Masefield was orphaned at an early age and educated in the merchant navy training ship *Conway*, where he began to study the seamanship that would inform his best writing. He served his apprenticeship in the merchant service before ill health drove him ashore. He then spent several years in the US doing menial jobs before he returned to England and took up writing.

He scored his first successes as a journalist but it was not long before his first poetical work, *Salt Water Ballads* appeared in 1902. In 1903 he married Constance de la Cherois Crommelin and they had a daughter and a son. His narrative masterpiece, *Reynard the Fox*, was published in 1919 and widely acclaimed for its vision of rural English life. Masefield was also a respected religious dramatist whose plays included *Good Friday, The Trial of Jesus* and *The Coming of Christ*. He was made Poet Laureate in 1930 by Ramsay Macdonald.

H.L. Mencken 1880–1956

American journalist, editor, and critic of considerable wit, Mencken hailed from Baltimore and started life working in his father's cigar factory. Renouncing duty for ambition, he became the youngest reporter on the *Baltimore Morning Herald* and within five years its editor-in-chief. Intellectually, Mencken was spreading his wings beyond the confines of Baltimore, doing book reviews for chic New York publications including *The Smart Set* of which he was co-editor.

Modelling himself as a critic of ideas and champion of modern short fiction, Mencken is remembered mostly for his writing in the *New Yorker*. A determined bachelor, Mencken lived happily in the house he grew up in until his mother died, then suddenly at the age of fifty married the writer Sarah Powell Haardt. Sadly Haardt died after only five years of marriage and Mencken returned to the family home. 'My own private code of ethics is superior to that of most Christians', he wrote in his preface to *A Treatise on the Gods*.

Henry Miller 1891–1980

One of the great American iconoclasts, Miller was a prodigious writer of cult status. He lived in Paris during the 1930s and wrote *Tropic of Cancer* and *Tropic of Capricorn* while conducting a literary/romantic affair with Anaïs Nin with whom he had an insatiable correspondence. *Cancer* and *Capricorn* were not published in America until the 1960s because of their blatant sexuality. Miller wrote scores of non-fiction books as well as poetry, though he is better known for his novels, *The Air-Conditioned Nightmare* (1945) and *The Rosy Crucifixion* trilogy (1965).

Miller once described twentieth-century progress as 'the great hoax . . . we are making life stale, flat and unprofitable every day in every way.' Five times married, Miller was a libertine, a mystic and a great enthusiast of fads and cults which were not hard to come by in Big Sur, California, where he lived happily until his death in 1980.

George Moore 1852–1933

Born in County Mayo, Ireland, Moore was groomed for the army until his father's death in 1870 set him free to live the life of a dilettante artist and writer in Paris. Moore was one of the first novelists of the Realist school to be noticed in England, most notably with *Esther Waters* (1894).

He sought exile in Ireland during the Boer War, returning to England in 1911 where he dedicated himself to writing memoirs and confessions including the *Hail and Farewell* trilogy in which he satirised his friendship with W.B. Yeats during the setting up of the Abbey Theatre in Dublin. Of the recurring themes in Moore's work, that of the death of Jesus reached its peak in the writing of *The Brook Kerith* in 1916. It is this book and *Heloise and Abelard* (1921) for which Moore is chiefly remembered.

Malcolm Muggeridge 1903–90

Journalist and sage, Muggeridge was born in Croydon and educated at Cambridge. He married Beatrice Webb's niece Kitty Dobbs in 1927 and together they lived an exciting and unsettled life, following the trajectory of Malcolm's career around the world, including stints in Egypt and the Soviet Union. Muggeridge was stationed in Laurenco Marques (Mozambique) during the Second World War and was honoured for serving the intelligence corps with the Legion of Honour and the Croix de Guerre.

As a journalist he worked on the staff of the *Manchester Guardian*, the *Daily Telegraph* and the *Evening Standard*. Between 1953 and 1957 Muggeridge was editor of *Punch*, but it was as an outspoken and often pious television personality that he drew the most attention. As a regular contributor to the BBC's *Panorama*, and host of his own series *Appointment With*, Muggeridge was never off screen or out of the headlines for long. His marriage to Kitty survived the tempests of Malcolm's affections and together they converted to Roman Catholicism in 1982.

John Middleton Murry 1889–1957

London-born writer and critic, Murry was educated at Oxford where, as editor of *Rhythm* and *Athenaeum*, he had a strong influence on the young intellectuals of the 1920s. He produced volumes of poetry, essays and criticism during this period, his major works included biographies of *Keats and Shakespeare* (1925), *William Blake* (1933) and his friend D.H. Lawrence (1931).

In 1918 he married the writer Katherine Mansfield and after her premature death from tuberculosis he produced posthumous collections of her letters and diaries as well as a biography. A committed pacifist, Murry was editor of *Peace News* from 1940–6 and spent his final years absorbed in agriculture, starting a community farm in Norfolk.

Beverley Nichols 1899–1983

Bristol-born Nichols was a prolific writer of tremendous range, tackling fiction and subjects as diverse as religion, travel, politics and gardening. He was educated at Marlborough and Oxford where he wrote his first novel *Prelude* and was editor of *Isis*. A great traveller, Nichols spent much of his life on the road but nevertheless managed to create a reputation as a daring and unusual interviewer for the *American Sketch* of which he was editor for a year.

At twenty-five he calmly wrote his autobiography and in 1929 lost all his money in the stockmarket crash. He returned to England and recouped his losses by writing bestsellers. He was a passionate, if confused, writer who managed simultaneously to urge and then renounce pacifism, defend God from anti-theologians and predict Oswald Mosley as England's destined leader. He admitted, 'I am posing all my life.'

Harold Nicolson 1886–1968

Harold Nicolson was born in Tehran where his father was the British Minister to Persia. He was educated at Wellington and Oxford and afterwards pursued a career in the Foreign Office. He retired from the Diplomatic Service in 1929, thereafter applying himself to literature and wrote acclaimed biographies of Verlaine, Tennyson and Byron among others.

Despite his numerous achievements, including a ten-year spell in Parliament where he sat from 1935 to 1945, Harold Nicolson is best remembered for his open marriage to Bloomsbury clan writer and Sapphic heroine Vita Sackville-West and for his contribution to the creation of their famous home and garden at Sissinghurst Castle in Kent.

Thomas Paine 1737–1809

Revolutionary philosopher and pamphleteer, Paine was born in Norfolk and spent his early life working variously as a corsetmaker, schoolmaster and sailor. He sailed for Philadelphia in 1774 where he published a best-selling pamphlet arguing for complete American independence, *Common Sense*.

After serving in the US army Paine returned to England in 1787 and wrote a book in support of the French Revolution, *The Rights of Man*. Arraigned for treason, Paine fled to Paris where he was imprisoned for offering the King asylum in the United States. It was while he was incarcerated that he wrote his celebrated work in favour of deism, *The Age of Reason*. He died in poverty in New York and was refused a place in the Quaker burial ground.

Dennis Potter 1935–94

Born in Gloucestershire and educated at Oxford, Potter worked as a journalist and TV critic before he started to write plays. Primarily a television dramatist, he was acclaimed for many of his controversial works including *Pennies from Heaven* (1978), *The Singing Detective* (1986) and *Lipstick on Your Collar* (1993). But it was his portrayal of a self-doubting Christ in *Son of Man* in 1959 that ruffled the most feathers. The same year he married Margaret Morgan and together they had one son and two daughters.

An outspoken and memorable figure, Potter acquired a reputation which seemed to hang as much on his ill health as his work. A lifelong sufferer of the psoriasis he portrayed so grotesquely *in The Singing Detective*, Potter died after a long struggle with cancer in 1994.

Paul Potts 1911–90

Best known for his memoir, *Dante Called You Beatrice*, Paul Potts was a left-wing bohemian in thrall to the pub scene of Soho and Fitzrovia. Raised in Canada but educated at Stonyhurst, Potts arrived on London's literary scene in 1933 where he made friends with George Orwell and Dylan Thomas, publishing his first book of verse, *Instead of a Sonnet*, in 1944. A staunch Zionist, Potts travelled to Palestine to witness the birth of the Jewish state, a trip that prompted his disenchantment with Zionism and which he recorded in his book *To Keep a Promise* (1970).

Aside from the odd book review for the *Sunday Telegraph* and the *Tablet* Potts' output was meagre and when *Dante Called You Beatrice* was chosen as an A-level English text in the 1970s, he described it as 'a solitary feather in a rather dilapidated cap'. He died in high style in 1990 by setting fire to his bed.

Ezra Pound 1885–1972

American-born poet, Pound was educated at the University of Pennsylvania before coming to England where he wasted no time in making a name for himself in London's literary circles. Regarded by T. S. Eliot as the creator of modern poetry, Pound's main work was *The Cantos*, a loosely knit series of poems published in instalments between 1930 and 1959.

In between times, Pound kept busy by moving to Italy and making pro-Fascist broadcasts in the early stages of the Second World War. After the war he was escorted back to the United States and indicted for treason then thrown into an asylum when he was judged to be insane. After his release in 1958 he returned to Italy.

John Cowper Powys 1872–1963

Derbyshire-born and educated at Cambridge, Powys, like many English writers, was ill at ease in his own country and spent many years crossing the Atlantic trying to decide where he belonged. In the end, after marrying in 1896, he settled in north Wales with his wife and their son.

Powys lacked the general recognition of his contemporaries and was known only for his novel *Weymouth Sands*. His work, like Lawrence's, was informed by the quality of the exile who returns home to find himself at odds with his society. A tortured and interesting figure, Powys produced many contemplative works exploring myth and spirituality, including the minor classic *Religion of a Sceptic*. In recent years there has been a major revival of interest in his work.

Kathleen Raine b. 1908

Poet and literary critic, Raine described her hometown of Ilford as 'a place for those who do not wish (or cannot be) fully conscious, because full consciousness would perhaps make life unbearable.' She escaped to Cambridge in the 1920s and entered into two short-lived marriages: the first to the poet Hugh Sykes Davies and the second to Charles Madge.

Raine sought solace in her work, which would prove her to be a highly talented poet. Her first volume, *Stone and Flower*, was published in 1943. She also went on to write an enormous body of literary criticism. Among her subjects were Yeats and David Jones, but her *magnum opus* was the exhaustive, two-volume study of William Blake, *Blake and Tradition*. At ninety she continues to write accomplished poems distinguished by their strong mythological and archetypal themes.

Simon Raven b. 1927

Novelist, critic and dramatist, Raven was educated at Charterhouse and Cambridge and is a fond recollector of his public school degradations. He served as an army captain in Kenya for four years before turning to writing at the age of thirty and producing an enormous body of work including his famous *Alms for Oblivion* sequence of novels and a dramatization of Frances Donaldson's *Edward VIII*, *Edward and Mrs Simpson*.

An eccentric bachelor, Raven lives in an almshouse for impoverished gentlemen in Smithfield, London, from where he looks back without remorse on a lifetime's commitment to debauchery.

Jean-Jacques Rousseau 1712–78

The famous philosopher, moralist and educational theorist was born in Geneva, son of a watchmaker. In a wandering life, hounded as a heretic, he nevertheless became an influential thinker, especially in France where his political thesis *The Social Contract* was revered by the revolutionists of thirty years later.

Similarly, *Emile*, a fictionalised tract on education, which exalted the young child as a 'noble savage' who should be taught by gentle encouragement rather than by discipline and rote, became a key text for modern educators. However, Rousseau's own five illegitimate children, by a hotel chambermaid whom he married late in life, were all despatched to an orphanage at birth.

John Ruskin 1819–1900

Writer and art critic, Ruskin was born in London and educated at Oxford. After graduating he met Turner whose painting he championed in his first critical work, *Modern Painters* (1843). Other works including *The Seven Lamps of Architecture* and *The Stones of Venice* followed, but it was Ruskin's social criticism and his Jeremiah-like attacks on Victorian materialism that earned him the status of prophet and moral guide.

In 1870 Ruskin became Professor of Fine Art at Oxford. He spent his later years founding educational institutions and working on his unfinished autobiography, *Praeterita*. Gandhi was said to have been influenced by Ruskin's *Unto this Last*, first published in 1860.

Bertrand Russell 1872–1970

Philosopher and mathematician of outstanding brilliance, Russell was born in Monmouthshire to a progressive earl, Viscount Amberley, and his wife Kate who both died before Russell was four. Raised by his grandmother and various members of an eccentric extended family, Russell left home to be educated at Cambridge and became a fellow of Trinity College in 1895. By the end of the century he had completed the first of his great works, *The Principles of Mathematics.*

Russell was married four times and had many love affairs including those with Lady Ottoline Morrell and the actress and pacifist, Colette O'Neil. In 1911 he met Wittgenstein, who influenced his thinking ever after. Russell worked furiously all his life, producing countless influential works, his most famous being *A History of Western Philosophy*, an immediate and lasting success on both sides of the Atlantic. Arguably the single most important influence on twentieth-century philosophy, Russell, an atheist, was awarded the Nobel Prize for Literature in 1950.

Vita Sackville-West 1892–1962

Poet, novelist and famous gardener, Vita was born at Knole in Kent, daughter of Lord Sackville, a descendant of one of the most ancient Norman families. She recorded life in the great house in her novel *The Edwardians*. Her poem, *The Land*, was awarded the Hawthornden Prize in 1927.

In 1913 she married Harold Nicolson in an arrangement which suited them both well and enabled her to conduct her literary and romantic affairs, most notably with Virginia Woolf and Violet Trefusis. A talented gardener, she restored the Tudor mansion of Sissinghurst in Kent with her husband.

Dorothy Sayers 1893–1957

Writer and Christian apologist, Dorothy Sayers was educated in Oxford, the place of her birth. Her father, the Revd Henry Sayers, was the headmaster of Christ Church Choir School. She began her career as a teacher and advertising copywriter, penning thrillers in her spare time. Her first book, *Whose Body?*, was published in 1923, and featured Lord Peter Wimsey, the hero of eight more novels including *Murder Must Advertise* and *The Nine Tailors*.

In 1926 Sayers married a well-known war correspondent, Captain Oswald Fleming, and they adopted a son. Frustrated by what she saw as the limitations of the twentieth-century novel, she turned her attention to critical, political and theological issues. Of her many works, it was her radio play *The Man Born to be King*, broadcast at monthly intervals between 1941 and 1942, which has endured.

Albert Schweitzer 1875–1965

Philosopher, musician, theologian and medical missionary, Schweitzer was born at Kaysersberg in Alsace and studied in Strasbourg, Paris and Berlin. It was Schweitzer who famously declared that he would dedicate his life to science and art until he was thirty, thereafter to serving humanity. A curate and eventually principal of the theological college at Strasbourg, Schweitzer wrote assiduously on the works of St Paul and *The Quest of the Historical Jesus* was published in 1906.

True to his vow, at the age of thirty he gave all this up to study medicine and in 1913 set out with his new bride for Lambarene in French Equatorial Africa where they set up a hospital to fight leprosy. Apart from the odd European lecture visit, Schweitzer stayed there for the rest of his life and was awarded the Nobel Peace Prize in 1952.

George Bernard Shaw 1856–1950

Playwright and controversialist, Shaw was born in Dublin and came to London in 1876, where he attached himself to the Fabian Society and became known as a journalist and critic. He wrote over forty plays, beginning with *Widowers' Houses* in 1892. *Candida, Man and Superman* and his 'religious pantomime', *Androcles and the Lion* soon followed.

Shaw is widely remembered as the author of *Pygmalion*, later adapted as the musical *My Fair Lady*, but his interests went beyond drama. His many interests included vegetarianism and the devising of a phonetic alphabet, which came to be known as Shavian. He was awarded the Nobel Prize for Literature in 1925.

Percy Bysshe Shelley 1792–1822

Sussex-born poet and revolutionary romantic, Shelley was educated at Oxford, but was expelled for writing a pamphlet, *The Necessity of Atheism*, in 1811. He eloped with Harriet Westbrook to Scotland where he came under the influence of William Godwin. Shelley wrote his anarchic poem *Queen Mab* during this time, before eloping again, this time with Godwin's daughter, causing the first Mrs Shelley to take her own life.

From 1818 he lived in Italy where he met Byron and wrote the bulk of his poetry and his verse drama *Prometheus Unbound*. He was drowned in the Bay of Spezia near Livorno.

Upton Sinclair 1878–1968

A prolific writer in many prose genres, Sinclair was born to an impoverished family in Baltimore and took to writing to pay his way through college. His convictions were radical for his time and many of his novels, such as *The Jungle* and *King Coal*, depict the iniquities of big business. Sinclair also promoted pacifism, education and telepathy, criticising organised religion as a tool of capitalism.

Stevie Smith 1902–71

Poet and novelist, Stevie Smith was born in Hull and educated in London where she worked for the same publishing firm for thirty years. During this time she began to experiment with poetry and fiction, resulting in the original and successful *Novel on Yellow Paper* in 1936. Her poems were published the following year in the collection, *A Good Time Was Had by All*.

Slowly, Smith acquired a reputation as a humorous and eccentric poet on serious themes and, while her novels were a good showcase for her talent, it was her poetry which perfected it. Often autobiographical, Smith's work is funny and poignant on the themes of love, Englishness, loneliness and manners. Having once considered the possibility and decided against it, Steve Smith never married and lived until her death with a much-loved aunt.

Wallace Stevens 1879–1955

Born in Pennsylvania and educated at Harvard, Wallace Stevens's mythical status can be attributed to the infrequency of his sparse publications. He published four poems pseudonymously in 1914, then occasional small volumes until his *Collected Poems* (1954), which won a Pulitzer Prize.

Stevens was an odd combination of lawyer and metaphysical poet whose work was concerned with the process of perception; he drew his influences from the French Symbolists and had a penchant for free verse.

Count Leo Tolstoy 1828–1910

Tolstoy was born into the nobility in the Tula province of Russia. He spent his early years enjoying a dissolute whirl in Moscow and St Petersburg while neglecting his studies. It was only upon joining his brother Nicolay in the Caucasus, where he later joined an artillery regiment, that Tolstoy's literary life began. His first publication, *Childhood* (1852), was a wild success and became the first part of an autobiographical trilogy.

In 1862 he married Sofya Behrs with whom he settled to devotional family life, producing thirteen children. After six years of hard toil, Tolstoy published *War and Peace* in 1869. Considered by many to be the greatest novel ever written, it is concerned with the fortunes of three families during Napoleon's invasion of Russia. His other masterpiece, *Anna Karenina* (1873) was the result of a moral and spiritual crisis for the author and led to his total immersion in Christian anarchism, giving away his estate and possessions. He died of pneumonia whilst fleeing the homestead after his excommunication by the Russian Orthodox Church.

Philip Toynbee 1916–81

Philip Toynbee started his rebellious career by running away from Rugby at the age of seventeen to join the fifteen-year-old Esmond Romilly in founding *Out of Bounds*, a magazine with the stated intent of causing a revolution in British public schools. Throughout the 1930s he was the third side of an idealistic triangle with Romilly and his future wife Jessica Mitford, the trio united by their pugnacious opposition to fascism and a heartfelt commitment to hedonistic living.

Inheriting the genes of his father, the historian Arnold Toynbee, and a mother from decadent aristocratic stock, Philip Toynbee was both high-minded and debauched. Bacchanalian exploits did not prevent him from achieving a distinguished career as both foreign correspondent and, later, literary critic for some thirty years on the *Observer*. Though he published a respectable number of books, he never succeeded in his oft-stated aim to be a major writer of experimental fiction. Six volumes of his autobiographical epic in verse *Pantaloon* remain unpublished.

His two marriages produced five children and towards the end of his life he founded a short-lived agricultural commune in Wales, at the same time becoming increasingly preoccupied with Christianity. He recorded his spiritual pilgrimage in *Part of a Journey* published shortly before his death from cancer in 1981, and in the posthumously published *End of a Journey*.

John Updike b. 1932

Poet, novelist and critic, Updike was born in Pennsylvania to a high-school mathematics teacher and educated at Harvard and Oxford before taking up writing, his first pieces appearing in the *New Yorker* magazine. Updike's novels are acute studies of contemporary American life, the best known being his *Rabbit* series of books, describing the rise and fall of a Pennsylvanian car salesman, Harry Angstrom.

Updike's other classics are his novel *Couples* (1968) and a volume of autobiography, *Self-Consciousness* (1989). His novel *The Witches of Eastwick* was made into a film starring Jack Nicholson. Twice married, Updike is a churchgoer, a fanatical golfer and the father of four children.

Paul Verlaine 1844–96

Poet of the sacred and profane, Verlaine was born in Metz, France, and educated in Paris where he swiftly fell in with the leading Parnassian writers of the age. He achieved recognition with his second book of verse, *Fêtes galantes* in 1869, but it is in part his torturous relationship with fellow poet Rimbaud which keeps his name alive today.

Verlaine left his family in 1872 to travel with Rimbaud, but they quarrelled furiously and in a drunken despair at Rimbaud's intention to leave him, Verlaine shot his lover in the wrist, an offence for which he served two years in prison. Whilst incarcerated he wrote *Romances sans paroles*. Upon leaving he converted to Catholicism and spent several years teaching French in English schools.

H.G. Wells 1866–1946

One of the most progressive thinkers and writers during the momentous events of the first part of the twentieth century, Wells was born in Bromley, Kent, and started life as an apprentice draper. He dabbled in teaching and studied biology in London before he made his name in journalism and literature. Real fame came in 1895 with the publication of his scientific fantasy *The Time Machine* and in 1898 with *War of the Worlds*. He was successful, too, as a writer of the comic novels, *Kipps* and *The History of Mr Polly* (later made into films).

Wells' real calling was as the writer of socio-political tomes including *Anticipations*, *A Modern Utopia* and *The Work, Wealth and Happiness of Mankind*.

In 1891 he entered into a short-lived first marriage to his cousin Isabel, falling in love and running off shortly afterwards with one of his students, Jane. They married and had two sons, but it was upon meeting Rebecca West in 1912 that he finally met his match. They had a son but never married. Often engaged in public controversy, Wells was a great socialist, member of the Fabian Society, agitator for world peace and the improvement of the lot of mankind.

Rebecca West 1892–1983

Born Cecily Isabel Fairfield in London, the novelist and critic Rebecca West was educated in Edinburgh and for a short time took to the stage, appropriating her *nom de plume* from the character she played in Ibsen's *Rosmersholm*. Rebecca West first made her name as the widely praised correspondent for the *Daily Telegraph* at the Nuremberg Trials.

Her works included studies of D.H. Lawrence, Henry James and St Augustine as well as her novels *The Thinking Reed* and *The Birds Fall Down*. She once described writing novels as 'like embroidery, one of those things that women are rather good at'. Her long association with H.G. Wells produced a son, the author and critic, Anthony West. She was created a dame in 1959.

Antonia White 1889–1979

The world of Kensington-born writer Antonia White was dominated by her life-long struggle with Catholicism and mental illness. At nine years of age her parents became Catholics, marking a sharp change in her education which led to feelings of isolation and separateness from her peers. At fifteen, to please her father, she wrote a novel exemplifying his religious beliefs. This act of devotion was to lead to her expulsion from the convent when it was discovered by the nuns. Her turbulent upbringing was detailed in her first and best-known novel, *Frost in May*.

A nervous breakdown after the annulment of her first marriage led to nine months in an asylum. A second marriage lasted only five years, but it was her third husband who encouraged her to write again, which she did though the remainder of her life was spent struggling with mental illness.

Oscar Wilde 1854–1900

Dublin born writer, Wilde is one of the most celebrated artists of his age, his reputation continually refreshed by a never ending stream of biographies. Educated at Trinity College, Dublin, and Oxford, Wilde wasted no time establishing himself as a great wit in the literary circles of London. His skilful writing was more than a match for his flamboyant manner and among his celebrated works are the novel, *The Picture of Dorian Gray* and plays, *Lady Windermere's Fan* and *The Importance of Being Earnest*.

He married Constance Lloyd in 1884 and had two sons, but it was his staunch defence of his right to love another man that has made him a figurehead for the gay movement. His recklessness earned him two years hard labour in gaol for homosexual practices. Nevertheless, this bleak period led to the writing of two of his most important works, *The Ballad of Reading Gaol* and *De Profundis*. He died in exile in Paris.

A.N. Wilson b. 1950

Journalist, novelist and biographer, Wilson was educated at Rugby and Oxford where he began to collect the prizes and acclaim that are the hallmark of his varied and prolific career. His first novel, *The Sweets of Pimlico*, was published in 1977 and has been followed by more than sixteen novels since, including his excellent series of novels, *The Lampitt Papers*.

Wilson's biographies include *Tolstoy*, *C.S. Lewis* and *Hilaire Belloc*. In his short life, Wilson has been a Roman Catholic, an Anglican and an atheist and is the author of books about Jesus and St Paul. Twice-married, Wilson is the father of three daughters, the latest having brought him 'deep Blakean joy'.

ACKNOWLEDGEMENTS

For permission to publish copyright material in this book grateful acknowledgement is made to the following:

ARNOLD BENNETT: from *My Religion* (Hutchinson, 1926), to A.P. Watt Ltd. on behalf of Mme V.M.Eldin; G.K. CHESTERTON: from *Orthodoxy* (Hodder & Stoughton, 1996) and *The Essential G.K. Chesterton* (Oxford University Press, 1987), to A.P. Watt Ltd. on behalf of The Royal Literary Fund; E.E. CUMMINGS: 'no time ago' from *Complete Poems 1904–1962*, edited by George J. Firmage (W.W. Norton, 1994), © 1991 by the Trustees for the E.E. Cummings Trust and George James Firmage, to the publisher; ARTHUR CONAN DOYLE: from *My Religion* (Hutchinson, 1926), © 1996 The Sir Arthur Conan Doyle Copyright Holders, to Jonathan Clowes Ltd., London, on behalf of Andrea Plunket, Administrator of the Sir Arthur Conan Doyle Copyrights; SHUSAKU ENDO: from *A Life of Jesus* (Paulist Press, 1973), © 1973 by Shusaku Endo, English translation © 1978 by Richard A. Schuchert, to Paulist Press Inc; ROBERT GRAVES: from *King Jesus* (Cassell, 1946) and *The Nazarene Gospel Restored* (Cassell, 1955), to Carcanet Press Ltd., D.H. LAWRENCE: from *Fantasia of the Unconscious* (Thomas Seltzer, 1922), to Laurence Pollinger Ltd. and the Estate of Frieda Lawrence

OTHER SOURCES

Allain, Marie Francoise, *The Other Man: Conversations with Graham Greene*, Bodley Head, 1983

Arnold, Matthew, 'The Proof from Miracles', *Literature and Dogma*, Macmillan, 1889

Ayer, A.J., *Thomas Paine*, Secker & Warburg, 1988

Bennett, Arnold, *My Religion*, Hutchinson, 1926

Boswell, James, *Life of Samuel Johnson*, London: 1791

Carpenter, Humphrey, *Dennis Potter: A Life*, Faber & Faber, 1998

Clarke, John Henry, *William Blake . . . on the Lord's Prayer. Including Blake's annotations on Dr. Thornton's translation of the Lord's Prayer*, Hermes Press, 1927

Collis, John Stewart, *Bound Upon a Course*, Sidgwick & Jackson, 1991

Conrad, Joseph, *Letters of Joseph Conrad*, Cambridge University Press, 1986

Cross, J.W., ed., *Life of George Eliot*, Blackwood, 1885

Davenport-Hines, Richard, *Auden*, Heinemann, 1995

Duran, Leopoldo, *Graham Greene: Friend and Brother*, HarperCollins, 1994

Ellis, Alice Thomas, *Home Life*, Akadine Press, 1997

Ellis, Havelock, *Impressions and Comments*, Constable, 1924

Ellis, Havelock, *Affirmations*, Constable, 1915

Gordon, Mary, *Incarnation, Contemporary Writers on the New Testament*, Viking, 1990

Heine, Heinrich, *Shakespeare's Maids and Women*, quoted in *England: An Anthology* ed., Richard Ingrams, HarperCollins, 1990

Hopkins, Gerard Manley, *Gerard Manley Hopkins*, ed.,Catherine Phillips, Oxford University Press, 1986

Hunt, Holman, 'The Real Jesus Versus the Idealised Christ of Pictorial Art' in *Pre-Raphaelitism and the Pre-Raphaelite Brotherhood*, vol. i., Macmillan, 1905

Hunter, Ian, *Malcolm Muggeridge: A Life*, Thomas Nelson, 1980

Huxley, Aldous, *Aldous Huxley Letters*, Chatto & Windus, 1969

Jefferies, Richard, *Richard Jefferies Notebooks*, Grey Walls Press, 1948

Keats, John, *Letters of John Keats*, ed., Maurice Buxton Foreman, Oxford, 1952

Lewis, Jeremy, *Cyril Connolly: A Life*, Jonathan Cape, 1997

Mailer, Norman, from *Waterstones Magazine*, 1977

Mencken, H.L., *Treatise on the Gods*, John Hopkins University Press, 1997

Miller, Henry, *Big Sur and the Oranges of Hieronymous Bosch*, William Heinemann, 1958

Miller, Henry, *Stand Still Like the Hummingbird*, New Directions, 1962

Millgate, M., ed., *The Life and Works of Thomas Hardy*, Macmillan, 1984

Moore, George, 'On Reading the Bible for the First Time', from the Introduction to *The Apostle*, Maunsel & Co, 1911

Murry, John Middleton, *The Life of Jesus*, Jonathan Cape, 1926

Nichols, Beverly, *The Fool Hath Said*, Jonathan Cape, 1936

Paine, Thomas, *The Age of Reason*, New York: 1794

Potts, Paul, *Dante Called You Beatrice*, Eyre & Spottiswoode, 1960

Potts, Paul, *To Keep a Promise*, MacGibbon and Kee, 1970

Powys, John Cowper, *The Pleasures of Literature*, Cassell, 1938

Raine, Kathleen, *Farewell Happy Fields*, Hamish Hamilton, 1973

Raven, Simon, interview with Naim Atallah, the *Oldie*, March 1998

Richardson, Joanna, *Verlaine*, Weidenfeld, 1971

Rousseau, Jean-Jacques, *Oeuvres*, Paris: 1793

Ruskin, John, *Modern Painters: Complete Edition*, George Allen, 1888

Russell, Bertrand, *The Enemy of Progress*, Routledge, 1975

Russell, Bertrand, *Why I Am Not a Christian and Other Essays on Religion and Related Subjects*, Routledge, 1992

Sackville-West, Vita, *This I Believe*, Hamish Hamilton, 1953

Schweitzer, Albert, *The Psychiatric Study of Jesus*, Beacon Press, 1950

Shelley, Percy Bysshe, *Shelley's Prose*, ed., D.L. Clark, University of New Mexico Press, 1954

Sinclair, Upton, *A Personal Jesus*, Allen and Unwin, 1954

Smith, Stevie, *Me Again: Uncollected Writings*, ed., Jack Barbara and William McBrien, Virago, 1983

Spater, George, *William Cobbett*, Oxford University Press, 1982

Stevens, Wallace, *Letters of Wallace Stevens*, Faber & Faber, 1967

Tolstoy, Leo, *What I Believe*, Oxford University Press, 1958

Toynbee, Philip, *End of a Journey*, Bloomsbury, 1988

Toynbee, Philip, *Part of a Journey*, Collins 1981

White, Antonia, *Diaries*, ed., Susan Chitty, Constable, 1992

Wilde, Oscar, *De Profundis*, Methuen, 1905

Wilde, Oscar, *The Soul of Man Under Socialism*, Arthur
  Humphreys, 1912
Wilson, A.N., *How Can We Know?*, Hamish Hamilton, 1985
Wilson, A.N., Introduction to *St Matthew's Gospel*, Canongate,
  1998